The Philosophy and Practice of Outstanding Early Years Provision

This book examines the philosophical and theoretical foundations of early years practice, and supports practitioners as they reflect on the collective and personal rationales which motivate and inform their work with young children. Theoretical underpinnings are explored from a variety of perspectives, and are translated into effective strategies for application in a range of early years settings.

Featuring contributions from leading early years professionals, *The Philosophy and Practice of Outstanding Early Years Provision* draws on sound expertise to deepen the reader's understanding of the concepts and ideas behind everyday practice. The book is divided into four easily navigated sections which explore key issues including the creation of enabling environments, leadership in the early years, the opportunities and challenges presented by diversity, and the value of creative approaches. Recommended strategies are discussed in relation to emerging global pressures and the needs of the contemporary child, inviting practitioners to modify and enhance future behaviour and practice.

This will be essential reading for students and practitioners who wish to improve current and future practice by gaining insight into the philosophical foundations which underpin outstanding provision.

Pat Beckley is Senior Lecturer in the School of Teacher Development at Bishop Grosseteste University, UK. She teaches across the undergraduate, early years teacher status, and postgraduate primary and MA in education courses, and supports work within the research modules and dissertations throughout these programmes.

The Philosophy and Practice of Outstanding Early Years Provision

Edited by Pat Beckley

Routledge
Taylor & Francis Group

LONDON AND NEW YORK

First published 2018
by Routledge
2 Park Square, Milton Park, Abingdon, Oxon OX14 4RN

and by Routledge
711 Third Avenue, New York, NY 10017

Routledge is an imprint of the Taylor & Francis Group, an informa business

© 2018 selection and editorial matter, Pat Beckley; individual chapters, the contributors

British Library Cataloguing in Publication Data
A catalogue record for this book is available from the British Library

Library of Congress Cataloging in Publication Data
Names: Beckley, Pat, editor.
Title: The philosophy and practice of outstanding early years provision /
edited by Pat Beckley.
Description: Abingdon, Oxon ; New York, NY : Routledge, 2018. |
Includes bibliographical references.
Identifiers: LCCN 2018003021 | ISBN 9781138635326 (hbk) |
ISBN 9781138635333 (pbk) | ISBN 9781315206431 (ebk)
Subjects: LCSH: Early childhood education. | Educational leadership. |
Multicultural education. | Creative ability–Study and teaching.
Classification: LCC LB1139.23 .P488 2018 | DDC 372.21–dc23
LC record available at https://lccn.loc.gov/2018003021

ISBN: 978-1-138-63532-6 (hbk)
ISBN: 978-1-138-63533-3 (pbk)
ISBN: 978-1-315-20643-1 (ebk)

Typeset in Optima
by Out of House Publishing

Printed and bound in Great Britain by
TJ International Ltd, Padstow, Cornwall

Contents

Acknowledgements

Grateful thanks go to the staff at Washingborough Primary Academy, particularly Jason O'Rourke, Headteacher, and Steve Baker, Chair of Governors, for their kindness in sharing their knowledge and understanding of the outstanding early years provision and their support during this project. Thanks also go to staff at Molescroft Primary School for the continued 'outstanding' work achieved and reflected upon.

About the contributors

Pat Beckley (editor)

Pat has worked in education for many years, initially as a Key Stage 2 coordinator and then for a long period leading an early years unit, particularly supporting children and families in challenging circumstances. As an 'outstanding teacher' with Advanced Skills Teacher status and a National Professional Qualification for Headship (NPQH), she supported early years settings and schools. Her work in higher education, where she became a Senior Fellow of the Higher Education Academy, involved leading early years and primary ITE programmes, participating in the design of national initiatives and conducting comparative research with colleagues in Africa and Europe, especially Norway.

Liz Creed

Liz is a CBT therapist with a background in psychology. Prior to her current role she worked as a psychological wellbeing practitioner within a National Health Service primary care setting and gained clinical experience with child and adolescent mental health services. She was awarded an MSc in Foundations of Clinical Psychology by the University of Wales, Bangor.

Karin Moen

Karin is Assistant Professor and former Head of Early Childhood Education at Hedmark University College, Hamar, Norway. She has extensive experience working with early years children, mainly in Norway but in England too.

Ami Montgomery

Ami leads the MA in TESOL at Bishop Grosseteste University. She taught in Manchester, where she held a variety of roles including spending a substantial amount of time teaching English to newly arrived children. Her doctoral study concerns the exploration of intercultural communication in the multicultural classroom.

Aimee Quickfall

Aimee is a Senior Lecturer at Bishop Grosseteste University, Lincoln. She works across the postgraduate and undergraduate teacher training courses. Previously, Aimee was a primary school teacher for twelve years, teaching in every year group from Nursery to Year 6. She is currently studying for a doctorate at Sheffield Hallam University, researching the experiences and career choices of women returning to teaching after becoming mothers.

Emma Revill

Emma studied geography at Plymouth University and trained to teach through a PGCE programme at Birmingham City University. She initially taught in London and moved to Lincoln. After teaching in primary age phases she became a Foundation Stage Leader, in a school where the Ofsted inspection in 2017 deemed the provision 'outstanding.'

John Stafford

John is programme development manager for soundLINCS and has wide-ranging expertise in playing instruments. He has had extensive musical experience throughout his career, supporting through his work in music groups such as early years providers, children with special needs, older age groups and those who are vulnerable.

Jonathan Wainwright

Jonathan is Principal Lecturer in Educational Leadership and Management at Sheffield Hallam University. He was a lead tutor for the National Professional Qualification for Integrated Centre Leaders (NPQICL). His doctoral study examined how children's centre leaders' professional and personal biographies have influenced their understanding and practice of leadership.

Foreword

Early years practice is highly complex and requires a deep understanding of issues to enable those working with young children to make informed decisions concerning the strategies they should devise, and implement, in an ever-changing environment. This book provides a rich account of philosophical perspectives, and resulting strategies, incorporated into relevant and high-quality practice. International, contemporary challenges and initiatives are introduced to encourage reflection and to inform outstanding early years practice. Strategies to enable young children to incorporate these reflections and their own ideas are also discussed. The young children's changing world is scrutinised through a diverse society lens, considering both leadership and a critical thinking approach. The book widens insights by considering the use of creativity, particularly music, and a love of nature and the outdoors. The final section of the book explores the wellbeing of the young child for life, assessment strategies to maintain the tracking of progress, and the different qualifications used when working with early years children. Contributors have extensive expertise in early years and are involved in collaboration with colleagues around the world, to include liaison with those undertaking international research. This ensures the book is most relevant to students, academics and all those working with young children.

Dr Nick Gee
Head of the School of Teacher Development
Bishop Grosseteste University
Lincoln

Introduction

'Philosophy,' from the Greek, means a 'love of wisdom.' This book seeks to encourage practitioners to think deeply about the philosophy underlying their provision for the babies and young children in their setting, and to consider their approach and personal rationale, while providing guidance for effective strategies in practice to promote children's own philosophical understanding of issues and happenings around them. The *Oxford English Living Dictionaries* (2017) state that philosophy is

> 1. The study of the fundamental nature of knowledge, reality, existence, especially when considered as an academic discipline; 1.1 A particular system of philosophical thought; 1.2 The study of the theoretical basis of a particular branch of knowledge or experience; 2 A theory or attitude that acts as a guiding principle for behaviour.

This book delves into the underlying principles of a philosophical approach that can be adopted in early years, and how this might influence practice for those involved with the care and education of babies and young children. The theoretical basis of such an approach is explored from a variety of viewpoints. Theories are considered to inform and act as guiding principles for a personal philosophical approach that practitioners involved or working with babies and young children can pursue. Trends, including global pressures that may influence how the early years are viewed, are scrutinised. Inherent power dynamics that may impact on practice through a need to follow directions or become technicians in the setting are discussed in terms of an awareness of philosophical foundations of practice that can give insights and knowledge. Michel Foucault (1926–1984), a French philosopher, challenged the belief that

> power crushes individuals while knowledge sets them free. Instead the two are closely implicated. Knowledge, or what is defined as legitimate knowledge, is a

product of power, but in turn acts as an instrument of power, playing a key role in the formation and constitution of disciplines.

(Dahlberg et al., 2002: 30)

Having awareness and knowledge gives practitioners a power over their work: it entails that they not only agree with what they are doing but know why they are doing it and what has caused it or brought it about.

Consideration is also given in this book to how philosophical ideas might be promoted for early years children, such as strategies to create an environment where children can explore, create, investigate, examine, take risks in their learning and value their achievements and those of others. The importance of creating a suitable space and giving adequate time is explored, as both are necessary to encourage children to develop the thinking skills and creativity needed to act on their own ideas. Children's sense of who they are, fostered through their own experiences and their responses to others' perceptions of them, impacts upon what they can do and achieve. Adults and young children are encouraged to build on their existing experiences to create new realities of understanding that can adjust and respond to changes and can be reviewed and reflected upon to shape future personal behaviour and practice.

Part 1 Philosophy for an enabling environment

Part 1 discusses the philosophy underlying the environments we construct for young children. Possible factors for reflection, concerning differences and similarities in the composition of an enabling environment, are covered, as is the question of how these might be influenced by international perspectives and local policy initiatives. Aimee Quickfall explores how a philosophical approach is cultivated in practice and deliberates on key issues. Jonathan Wainwright considers the role of leadership within such an environment and how this can further enhance practice.

Part 2 Diversity and diverse philosophical ideas

Part 2 concerns how diversity and diverse thinking can inform the nature of the setting and promote broad understandings. Ami Montgomery considers how a multicultural setting operates and what factors should be addressed in reflections on practice. Pat Beckley describes strategies that can be adopted at settings to encourage children to use creating and thinking skills, along with sustained shared thinking between children and adults. Key theories that influence thinking about learning and teaching approaches are discussed.

Part 3 Philosophical perspectives for creativity

Part 3 begins with a focus on a setting in England deemed 'outstanding.' The chapter by Emma Revill and Pat Beckley explores how the setting promotes independent thinking through creativity. John Stafford explores how he has used a philosophical understanding of the vital nature of music and sounds to engage babies and young children by promoting early awareness of such aspects as rhyme and pitch. He describes the many programmes he has successfully used to aid practitioners working with this age phase. Karin Moen uses her wealth of expertise to give insights into a love of nature and how this can be cultivated at settings, and considers similarities and differences between settings in the UK and Norway.

Part 4 Wellbeing as a foundation for philosophy

Part 4 opens with an argument by Liz Creed for the role of wellbeing as a factor in promoting the use of philosophical reasoning. Key theories are described with reference to how they relate to early years practice. Pat Beckley describes some aspects of the complex roles of early years practitioners and how philosophy can be incorporated into their practice. Finally, challenges for the future are considered in terms of a postmodern perspective on experiences, change and reflection. Through cultivating philosophical understanding practitioners and children can learn to value their own thoughts, opinions and ideas, a process which can support their endeavours throughout their lives.

Further reading

Hall, K. Murphy, P. Soler, J. (2008) *Pedagogy and Practice: Culture and Identities* London: Sage.

References

Dahlberg, G. Moss, P. Pence, A. (2002) *Beyond Quality in Early Childhood Education and Care: Postmodern Perspectives* London: RoutledgeFalmer.
Oxford English Living Dictionaries (2017) Philosophy. https://en.oxforddictionaries.com/definition/philosophy.

Part 1

Philosophy for an enabling environment

The contemporary early years world

Pat Beckley

Overview

This chapter considers how similar and different approaches can be implemented in a variety of ways in diverse contexts. Philosophical understandings influence the policies that are designed and the provision devised. The chapter discusses which factors might influence provision for early years and how ideas that work in particular contexts are shared but changed to fit the needs of different contexts. Issues that are affected by closer global networks are considered, such as safeguarding measures, partnerships with parents and technological advances. A networking and sharing of ideas, leading to a convergence of views, is explored and considered in terms of practical application to the needs of early years settings.

Introduction

The chapter opens by detailing philosophies that might have had an impact on provision for early years children in the contemporary world. Facilities and approaches to support children and the adults involved in their care and education in the early years continue to change as knowledge and understanding of this age phase develops and responds to new thoughts and findings. At a macro level, policies setting frameworks or guidelines for practitioners to follow can set requirements for personal, social and emotional development, physical development, health, understanding of mathematics, literacy and the wider world, language and creativity. These could be taken to have various strands, such as historical and geographical knowledge about the locality and art, music or dance. Frameworks may also specify for example a knowledge of local culture or an understanding of a second language.

International perspectives

Many theoretical perspectives explore how cultures and societies have been influenced by the wider world. Ideas may be shared globally, as suggested by Waters (1995: 3), who describes globalisation as 'a social process in which constraints of geography on social and cultural arrangements recede and in which people become increasingly aware that they are receding.' Lauder et al. (2008: 4) also considers the implications of adopting a whole-world picture, arguing that 'it is a world of collective consciousness, where we see our problems as interconnected.' In provisions conceived as part of a global view, early years settings would need to respond to global initiatives and assessments, such as league tables.

Gammage (2006: 235) raises the importance of early years discussions at national levels, stating 'In the twenty-first century it is probably evident to every parent, professional childcare worker, kindergarten and primary teacher that early childhood is high on the political agenda almost everywhere.' The particular perspective on early years that any framework or practitioner adopts can affect how early years provision is observed and implemented: for example, Cole (2008: 28) considers a Marxist perspective on global practice. This standpoint could have implications for understanding the early years as a means to provide a future workforce. A Marxist observer might ask, would the delivery of activities encourage a compliant workforce, ready to acquiesce to working conditions offered?

There are suggestions that global forces take the form of 'McDonaldisation,' whereby early years provision becomes similar and standardised. Ritzer (1996: 79) suggests that a McDonaldised society expects standardised 'order, systemization, formulation' and 'routine.' Yet McDonaldisation could in turn cause a backlash where people wish to hold on to what is perceived as an identity, such as was the case with the 2016 Brexit vote in the United Kingdom. Thus early years settings may respond by adopting a prescribed format or a specific theme, such as an outdoor facility or key theorist approach, to gain an identity.

Bryman (2004: 2) gives another perspective on global influences. He suggests a 'Disneyization' could occur as global standardisation 'rides roughshod over local cultures and practice.' He claimed 'Disneyization' could be 'the process by which the principles of the Disney theme parks are coming to dominate more and more sectors of American society as well as the rest of the world.' However, early years practitioners can interpret national policies and initiatives within their own philosophical understanding and implement them according to their values, adhering to broad guidelines. This will be discussed further in Chapter 11, based on a study of the adults working with the child.

Cerny (2007: 2) considers the effects of globalisation to generate a possible conflict, where there are two sorts of boundaries: *vertical* boundaries, concerned with physical or territorial locations, and *horizontal* boundaries which cover social stratification and differing mores. Accommodating this conflict in early years provision would require early years practitioners to 'shoehorn the horizontal into the vertical,' through attempts to implement macro-scale policies in existing local provision. Within the complex role of early years practitioner there exists a challenge to devise strategies whereby macro policies are accommodated within the local remit. For example, in Norway the national desire for assessments is located by practitioners in existing outdoor provision, and in England early years practitioners design strategies to satisfy their colleagues' need for assessments in classes including older children, while still providing an appropriate learning environment for the young children in their care.

International challenges to early years provision

Waters (1995: 124) suggests there are three forms of globalisation: economic, political and cultural. Historically, macro systems have been affected by trade, nation-state negotiations and the sharing of ideas. In the 17th–19th centuries there emerged the political states that would in the contemporary world appear to be increasing in strength, together with tighter border controls. Yet those apparently firm boundaries are in fact blurred through the shrinking world brought about by high-speed transport links, instant internet communication and common concerns regarding environmental issues. According to Woodhead (2006), 'Early education is now part of the process of globalisation through networking and sharing ideas and practice.' Prospective headteachers in England have been encouraged by the National College for School Leadership (NCSL) to consider approaches used in other countries:

> Our children will become world citizens. The similarities between issues for education within a similar economic and developmental framework are appreciable whilst our cultural differences can bring new thoughts to approaches to development in our countries.
>
> (Anonymous, NPQH Think Piece, National College for School Leadership, 2006)

Early years finances

Global economic concerns impact on early years provision with a need to keep a tight rein on costs, as well as to consider strategies that will provide early education to cultivate a new and economically viable workforce. These strategies may feature an emphasis on either core subjects or a broad range of learning areas to support thinking, and will require decisions on how to train those involved in working with young children, possibly 'on the job.' The United Nations International Children's Emergency Fund (UNICEF) in 2002 urged: 'no nation today can afford to ignore opportunities for maximising investments in education in a competitive economic environment based on knowledge, flexibility and lifelong learning' (Dahlberg and Moss, 2007: 5).

Children may need to develop skills which fit them for a new age, one characterised by technological knowledge and flexibility in outlook (See Chapter 5 for further discussion of this aspect). Developing the skills needed for the change from an industrial base to one demanding creativity could be the key to gaining employment in an increasingly competitive world where the workforce need to continually upgrade their skills and understanding to gain employment. These skills would need to be identified in early years provision and training in them implemented by practitioners.

The provision for early years reflects social changes in response to economic factors. Fukuyama (1996: 9) notes that 'economics is grounded in social life and cannot be understood separately from the larger question of how modern societies organise themselves.' In the present economic climate, parents may also need to have employment and may place demands for extended early years provision to accommodate this. This would intersect with social welfare concerns, with further challenges raised by an increasing older population requiring care. Ageing populations put further demands on workers to provide for them financially, and also demand welfare state assistance – at the possible expense of early years provision. In the scrutiny of financial considerations, resulting pressures could mean increased emphasis on the value obtained for the finances spent. This may be demonstrated in an interest in 'outcomes,' where specific aspects can be identified to show that the early years provision is providing value for money. In turn practitioners would be under pressure to deliver provision that satisfied such requirements, at the risk of losing the facility. The use of external regulators has significant implications for the viability of individual settings and for those who work there, pressurising them to conform to requirements and spend time providing evidence that this has been done. Funding tied to results obtained by external regulators, which are shared widely in subsequent reports, is vital if settings are to continue operating, given that parents and carers can easily move their children to those settings deemed to be more successful by the regulators. Some settings, even despite providing excellent provision, may be required to close if the funding required to sustain them is felt to be too great.

Reflections

What economic factors have influenced your involvement with young children – for example such considerations as the need for early years childcare while in employment, extended hours, being at home with a toddler, reference to cost of care when choosing a setting, the crucial nature of securing employment to meet the basic needs of an infant, the cost of professional training or resources for an early years setting?

How did that impact on the young child or children?

Political policy into practice

Government policy guidelines and frameworks may make reference to partners and the networks involved in formulating them, which may devise policies along similar lines. In a more constrained economic environment governments may tighten their structures to ensure value for money. Musgrave (1965: 240) stated 'Those in power are ensuring through the system that they maintain or have set up that pupils become persons of a certain type and this keeps society going as it is now.' Settings have responsibility for delivering guidelines, in ways that are measured to ascertain the provision's value: providers may then be required to change their practices to remain viable in a competitive market and meet the demands of the regulators who assess them. Competition for staff, resources and the children who come to the setting mean time and effort need to be spent on 'selling' the setting to the local community, at the expense of time spent on other aspects of the learning and development of the children. Competition between settings can be fierce as providers seek to maintain a sustainable facility with sufficient children to make it viable.

Reflections

Have you been involved in a competitive market for young children, either as a parent gaining a place for your child or as a practitioner in a setting?
What impact did it have on you and your child or the children? How did you feel about it and were any steps taken?

Early years cultural networks

Those interested in the learning and development of early years children have access to numerous networks and organisations where experiences and knowledge can be discussed and shared. Members of such bodies invariably seem to share an understanding which transmits readily to others. This understanding represents an ever-changing breadth of thinking that is shared, adapted to fit the context, and which then evolves and is shared again. Common views about experiences in settings and with babies and toddlers can be disseminated and critiqued to further enhance existing provision. Delivery is constantly being revised through new macro initiatives but also through practitioner interactions concerning knowledge and enhancements: see for example the spread of the 'forest school' approach for outdoor learning in England.

Global organisations influence practice by emphasising aspects such as literacy or technology, with a drive for outcomes that is shared internationally. Countries too share policies and practice in a way that affects those working with young children in those countries, for example in collaboration between Nordic countries or across the European Union. Questions concerning such factors as quality of provision and pedagogical bases are discussed, influencing policies and practice. This can lead to an uneasy interaction between diverse societies and convergent practice, where cultures seek to implement strategies, for example to raise standards in one area, in different contexts and within different social, cultural and physical environments.

Technological developments and the use of the internet have led to a swift communication of ideas through international networks. Cerny coins the phrase 'glocalisation' to identify the 'transnational epistemic communities of experts and professionals' who play a crucial role across the world in spreading transnational and global knowledge and organisational forms (Cerny, 2007: 15). In Europe these can include networks for those concerned with the care and education of young children, such as the European Early Childhood Education Research Association (EECERA). Clusters of interested parties in a locality can foster networking groups, such as young parents and carers groups, and school clusters – for example those concerned with tracking children's progress or with an aspect of an early years framework.

Case study

Ugandan early years teachers sought to support their children to learn English as a second language. Initially this was achieved through work with items, for example fruit was described in two languages or pieces of furniture labelled with the English name. A visit by two of the teachers to other settings secured a structured programme for the children to become fluent readers and speakers in English. This was successfully incorporated into activities within the setting to provide hands-on and relevant experiences for the children.

A learning area devised by the practitioner (Figure 1.3) uses made resources from natural materials. They could be used for such activities as an investigation of natural material properties, time, sounds, shapes or number.

Figure 1.1 An English setting with stimulating activities, taken by Pat Beckley when visiting a Nottinghamshire school, 2017

The Ugandan classroom has approximately thirty children who are seated around tables with a Blackboard at the front of the room for formal activities. The children have allocated active sessions outdoors during the day, incorporating music and physical games, along with an afternoon nap on mattresses in another room.

Reflections on practice

Consider a different approach from your own that may have given you opportunities to change your thinking (see Figures 1.1, 1.2 and 1.3).
How was this demonstrated in your practice towards young children?
What differences did it make to the children's understandings of a wider world?

Figure 1.2 A Norwegian early years setting exploring the outdoors, taken by Pat Beckley when visiting Hamar, Norway, 2017

International organisations

Macro drivers from international recommendations also influence early years provision, including input from such organisations as the United Nations Convention on the Rights of the Child (UNCRC), the World Bank, the Organisation for Economic Co-operation and Development (OECD) and the European Commission. Rationales for designing outcomes frameworks will vary according to the remit of the organisation; for example the UNCRC may focus on the voice of the child, while the World Bank may consider financial implications. International league tables, such as the OECD Programme for International Student Assessment (PISA), reinforce a competitive nature for provision, prompting discussion of aspects such as wellbeing or literacy and driving scrutiny of why some national policies may appear to be more effective than others.

For children in the contemporary world, what new prospects and challenges lie ahead? A shrinking world may mean that they are fortunate to have opportunities to travel the world and learn about other cultures and contexts at first hand. Yet those who have travelled because of necessity, due to problems in their birth country, may be traumatised by

Figure 1.3 A learning space in a Ugandan early years classroom, taken by Pat Beckley when visiting a nursery in Rugungiri, Uganda, 2017

their experiences and require expert, sensitive understanding to support their relocation. Language challenges can be overcome through strategies such as seeking another child or adult who can speak the language, a 'buddy' system or pictorial prompts, but care must also be taken to ensure the child is working at their optimal level of attainment, despite learning a new language. Travel might also occur for the purpose of visiting relatives abroad or to accompany parents as they travel for their jobs. A multi-cultural, diverse society enables young children to be aware of different cultures and develop wide perspectives and understandings. This can be built upon in early years practice by planning opportunities for children to broaden their experiences. Visits to the locality and an awareness of where they are, either where their home is located or school is situated, can begin to help children gain an understanding of their place in the world. Shops, visitors, themes – for example Indian dance or a Chinese physical activity – can support their widening outlook. Social welfare systems and infrastructures may seek to ensure children have enough to eat, are housed and can access health care. Other opportunities for children mean that the world can appear an exciting, welcoming place to be, where they are surrounded by families and networks that love and care for them.

Convergence of practice

Countries may have similar early years policies, for example sharing an emphasis on the importance of the first language as a means of communication, but these policies may be implemented in vastly differing ways according to the cultural foundations within the country. A setting in England is discussed in Chapter 7, demonstrating the creativity in activities and in the children's responses encouraged there. The philosophical perspective in Norway and the importance of the Norwegian love of the outdoors is explored in Chapter 9. Settings in the two countries have exchanged ideas and the forest school approach is being introduced rapidly in settings in England, while the Norwegian government is set to introduce assessments along the lines of those used in England. This convergence of policy, yet with adjustments to suit the context in which the policy is applied, demonstrates the sharing of ideas arising from dissimilar background contexts. In Uganda the 'Education for All' policy demonstrated a desire to enable all children to learn, become literate and achieve employment, which in turn would benefit the country through the economic prosperity a highly skilled workforce would bring. Published literacy schemes from England were observed in action and then adopted, with modifications.

Case study

A workshop was arranged in an early years class in Uganda, to share among practitioners from Uganda, England and Norway experiences of working with young children. The Ugandan class was part of a school and nursery established in a relatively remote part of the country to help the children in the local community. It had humble beginnings in a corrugated iron shed but quickly expanded, through government finance and sponsorship, to become a well respected institution in the locality, with approximately five hundred children attending. The school was approached by a dirt-track road which was due to be upgraded in the future. Internet, electricity and water access were intermittent. The nursery team were keen to improve the facility for their children and eager to learn of new initiatives which could be incorporated into their practice. Each of the five classes accommodated thirty to thirty-five children aged two to six; these numbers were lower than national official recommendations.

The staff were fascinated by the Norwegian model, although they felt it was not safe to let the children roam and there was a high wall and gate to keep them safe within the nursery compound. The practitioners, who all spoke fluent English, listened carefully to the ideas discussed and suggested approaches that they themselves used. The Ugandan practitioners had incorporated phonics practise and devised an outdoor play area for use at specific times of the day, along with action movements, dancing and music. There were limited resources available but the practitioners used natural resources to support learning.

Internationalised societies

While global markets can herald heightened competition from workers in other countries, they also provide opportunities for people to travel with their families and establish a home away from the place of birth. Our diverse, internationalised society brings a breadth of understanding of the world drawn from those around us, strengthening communities and their ability to encourage new ideas and gain a knowledge of different ways of perceiving events.

Partnerships with parents/carers

Partnerships between parents/carers and childcare settings or school are crucial for the positive development of the young child. Initial discussions at the earliest stages can support tracking of children's development and help to identify possible issues that may need further support and strengths which can be developed. This can start a shared dialogue that persist throughout a child's time accessing the provision. It means parents or carers and adults working with the child have shared understandings of the child; this will be reflected in relationships with that child, who will be reassured that those concerned with him or her are working together. Parents or carers' knowledge of their child is crucial, particularly in the early stages, to help practitioners get to know individual children quickly and ensure there is no mismatch between expectations and what the child can do. Any transitions can be managed to create a smooth change that is not distressing for the child. This can be enhanced through collaborative activities or by keeping parents or carers informed about tasks, projects and themes in the setting, any support they might be able to give and special occasions planned. Achievements and special events can be celebrated by all.

These discussions suggest an easy collaboration between partners but in practice the situation may be complex. In a workshop in Uganda between English and Ugandan colleagues consideration was given to the role of parents in their children's education. Views differed between colleagues in the two countries. Some felt the liaison should be as described in the previous paragraph, while others suggested strongly that it was the role of educators to be responsible and accountable for the educational progress of the children: they were the professionals. A heated debate included arguments that the parents have their child's best interests at heart and should raise their child as they see fit. Others suggested an early years or school environment can provide a way of living which can be adhered to and that follows agreed national guidelines.

Perhaps there is a professional way to deal with parental partnerships. I was reminded of cases in England where a mother proudly displayed her new dress which her son had stolen for her or the Ofsted inspection where a boy 'held up' the inspector and asked for her money. When told this is not the way we behave the child responded, 'My dad does.' An abusive household at home will also require measured interventions. In such cases an appropriate, welcoming environment can provide another way of living, giving children a calm, secure basis to learn and grow. Children can learn how such an environment works from an early age, although it might be different from what they experience at home. Epstein et al.'s (2002) continuum of partnership includes three models: a protective model, along a business partnership pattern; a school-to-home transmission model, where discussion follows a setting-to-home pathway; and a curriculum enrichment model, which incorporates collaboration and the partnership model (cited in Fitzgerald 2004: 24).

Multi-agency working

Working in partnerships is a key aspect of effective practice. Pupil premium provision, granted to support eligible pupils to reach levels of attainment appropriate to their abilities, is carefully considered to ensure resources are available. Those needing further support, through such agencies as either social work, speech and language therapy or physiotherapy, will be allocated support following team discussions to assess the appropriateness of an intervention. Such partnerships are a key aspect to ensure the delivery of high-quality learning and development for all children, irrespective of need. Practitioners work together across services and during transitions. The agencies concerned go beyond health, social care and education and may include library, music, artistic or other agencies deemed beneficial to enhance the life chances of individuals. There are challenges to the arrangement when different language forms are used in different agencies: care must be taken to avoid misunderstandings. It is important too to allocate sufficient time to involve parents fully in decisions about their child.

In early years settings practitioners often have a range of professional backgrounds, with knowledge of young children gained through childminding, healthcare, education or nursery facilities to name a few. This provides a useful combination of different perspectives as a basis for shared discussions. As in all early years teamwork, respectful and valued contributions from all participants in discussions promote optimal outcomes for the children who are being supported.

Technology

Technological advances and the use of the internet promote the notion of a shrinking world. Adults and the children in their care are able to access others from around the world: children might speak through Skype to grandparents on the other side of the world, and adults involved with early years might collaborate remotely through webinars. Increasingly young children have access to technological tools, particularly in more affluent countries, and learn to use them readily through frequent exposure. Settings incorporate digital resources in their children's play, for example Beebots allow children to rehearse such skills as planning, mapping, counting, recognising shapes and numbers and designing routes; other technologies might offer language and sound games or let children practise with handwriting or maths programmes. Children can learn about the world by searching for internet resources. Devices from games to small surveillance points are becoming increasingly familiar. Early years practitioners demonstrate a range of expertise with technological tools, with some settings being amazed by an iPad while others undertake complex activities such as matching a code on a piece of work to one displayed on an iPad, which could then display a variety of resources, for example research undertaken on a variety of elements of a project.

Case study

International links among a group of nurseries initially encouraged children to learn about aspects of the countries involved, for example the national flags. This quickly developed into sharing similarities in ways of living across borders, such as by comparing playing football in the grassed area in the centre of a circle of houses, hanging washing to dry on roofs overlooking the Mediterranean or by windows looking onto snowy mountains, or having a sleep in the afternoon. The comparison gave the children insights into different ways of living that they shared with other welcoming, friendly young children.

Games using the internet can be entertaining and maintain interest for children with their fast pace. Unfortunately they can also become addictive and adult care should be taken to check children's use. Overdependency on the computer rather than a balanced set of activities could lead to difficulties in interacting with peers. Children may become experts with digital games but lack social and personal skills, such as empathy, as this area is neglected in favour of computer games. There is a growing awareness too of the crucial role of safety and security when using the internet, and this aspect forms part of safeguarding procedures.

Safeguarding

The measures for safeguarding children are wide-ranging. At home aspects would broadly include assessing the safety of the adult who is with the child, but also managing health and safety risks, such as electricity, staircases, water storage or sources of heat. In 2008 the Department for Children, Schools and Families (DCSF) published guidelines comprising three areas: universal safeguarding, targeted safeguarding and responsive safeguarding. Meeting these guidelines required maintaining safe environments, including secure access; maintaining an appropriate space for all children, including those with special educational needs and vulnerable children; and responding swiftly if there is danger of harm. The Department for Education (DfE 2016: 5) guidelines *Keeping Children Safe in Education* emphasise that 'Safeguarding and promoting the welfare of children is everyone's responsibility. Everyone who comes into contact with children and their families and carers has a role to play in safeguarding children. The document continues 'Staff members working with children are advised to maintain an attitude of "it could happen here" where safeguarding is concerned.' The abuse could cover physical, emotional or sexual abuse or neglect. There should be specific structures within a setting to deal promptly with any issues that may arise.

Children in a contemporary world

Early years children in the contemporary world are facing new challenges. An ever-increasing population could mean difficulties in securing employment for adults, affecting children through such issues as poverty. Sedentary lifestyles, where a child may be less active and confined to working at a desk from a young age, can lead to health problems such as obesity and poor muscle development. In the context of competitive markets, children may experience a competitive dynamic in their group education, with adults perhaps applying pressure for success and peer pressure being exerted through comparisons of attainment and later possible negative technological encounters. There may be pressure to wear clothing with the 'correct' logo. These demands and challenges could lead to mental health issues. Constant changes, such as parental moves or migration, either to pursue work or escape war-torn areas, could result in many transitions for the child, leading to anxiety when attempting to gain an understanding of their surroundings, and to confusion about the different approaches, contexts and educational expectations encountered in each setting (see Chapter 10 for further discussion of wellbeing).

Brown states:

> One challenge is therefore to provide a space for children that will both inform them and allow them to develop for an unknown future. Thus a current challenge is to provide children with a positive childhood experience at a time when the economic climate nationally and internationally is somewhat unstable.
>
> (Brown and White, 2014: 13)

The following chapter considers how this can be achieved in an early years setting through a philosophical approach, where children use this perspective to develop their own independent ideas and rationales for them.

References

Brown, M. A. White, J. (2014) *Exploring Childhood in a Comparative Context* Abingdon: Routledge

Bryman, A. (2004) *The Disneyization of Society* London: Sage

Cerny, P. G. (2007) Neoliberalism and Place: Deconstructing and Reconstructing Borders in Arts, B. van Houtum H. Lagendijk A. *State, Place, Governance: Shifts in Territoriality, Governmentality and Policy* Berlin: Springer

Cole, M. (2008) *Marxism and Educational Theory: Origins and issues* London: Routledge

Dahlberg, G. Moss, P. (2007) *Ethics and Politics in Early Childhood Education* London: RoutledgeFalmer

Department for Education (2016) Keeping Children Safe in Education. https://www.gov.uk/government/uploads/system/uploads/attachment_data/file/550511/Keeping_children_safe_in_education.pdf

Epstein, J. L. Saunders, M. G. Simon, B. S. Salinas, K. C. Jansorn, N. R. Van Voorhis, F. L. (2002) *School, Family, Community: Your Handbook for Action* Washington: Office of Educational Research and Improvement

Fitzgerald, D. (2004) *Parent Partnerships in the Early Years* London: Continuum

Fukuyama, F. (1996) *Trust* London: Penguin Books

Gammage, P. (2006) *Early Childhood Education and Care: Politics, Policies and Possibilities* TACTYC, Colchester: Routledge

Lauder, H. Lowe, J. Chawla-Duggan, R. (2008) *Primary Review Interim Report. Aims for Primary Education; Changing Global Contexts* Cambridge: University of Cambridge

Musgrave, P.W. (1965) *The Sociology of Education* London: Methuen

National College for School Leadership (2006) *NPQH Think Piece* Booklet produced by the author

Ritzer, G. (1996) *The McDonaldisation of Society* London: Pine Forge Press

Waters, M. (1995) *Globalisation* London: Routledge

Woodhead, M. (2006) Changing Perspectives on Early Childhood: Theory, research and policy Background paper for prepared for the Education for All Global Monitoring Report 2007, Strong Foundations: Early childhood care and education: United Nations Educational, Scientific and Cultural Organisation

2 | Philosophy in the early years foundation stage
Playing with ideas

Aimee Quickfall

Overview

In this chapter I share my experiences of using philosophical inquiry with young children, give an overview of some of the debate around using philosophical inquiry and provide some practical advice and tools that you can used in your own setting or classroom. You may be an experienced practitioner, a trainee, one of our superhero teaching assistants or nursery workers or you might be an interested parent. The chapter is suitable for anyone involved with early years children.

Using philosophical inquiry in the EYFS

Philosophy can be a tricky word to define (and to say, especially for young children!), as many philosophers through history have admitted (Lacey, 1976). My teacher trainees recently described their idea of what a philosopher is, by drawing portraits of your average, everyday philosopher (see Figure 2.1).

Have a go at this now – or picture a philosopher in your 'mind's eye.'

What did you imagine? My trainees predominantly drew white men with beards and serious faces. Did your philosopher appear in a toga? I would be very pleased if we could change this perception and if the teaching trainees of future years could confidently draw themselves when set the same task. That is not to say I would like to erase Plato, Aristotle or Kant from our minds and studies, but perhaps treating our own thoughts and thought processes with respect would make us, as the great ones theorised, happier, more self-aware or perhaps better members of society.

A little about me – I have been using philosophy with children since I qualified as a teacher in 2004. I am, for my sins, a 'trained philosopher.' I studied for a philosophy degree and learnt about the grand masters (and yes, they were mostly men with beards) of western thinking, from Descartes to Wittgenstein. I know what you may be thinking – it

Figure 2.1 A white male philosopher, with obligatory facial hair
Photograph by Aimee Quickfall, 2017

is okay for her, she has a degree in philosophy, of course she thinks it is a good idea to teach this in settings and schools…but give me a chance! A degree in philosophy is perhaps more of a hindrance than a help when considering this as a subject for the early years of life. My training was in formal logic, epistemology, metaphysics and other long and potentially distressing words. If you enjoy teaching and especially *learning* with children and babies, then you are probably already doing some philosophy with them. My aim in this chapter is to help you refine your practice in this area, and to know when it is happening so you can better understand and celebrate the wonderful thinking that is going on.

In addition, I am not the only person to think philosophy is a valuable part of formal education (and life, but let's stick to school for now). In an extensive research study (Education Endowment Foundation, 2015 and also Gorard, Siddiqui and See, 2017), it was shown that introducing a session of philosophical inquiry for one hour a week in Key Stage 2 classes improved outcomes in reading, writing and mathematics. So far, so good, I hear you say…but consider the fact that a typical inquiry session with Key Stage 2 involves very limited writing and reading activity (perhaps a few words, to formulate a question) and almost certainly doesn't include any mathematics (or at least, not the kind of mathematical thinking that is measured in current statutory assessment tests). Teachers involved in the research reported that children had improved patience, listening skills and self-esteem over the year, too (Siddiqui, Gorard and See, 2017). The processes of forming a community of inquiry, discussing, questioning, reflecting and summarising had benefitted the diverse participant group of 3,000 students in many ways, both social and academic.

I have recently shared the findings of this research with my wonderful teacher trainees, who were shocked. They had been on placements in schools and, in a cohort of over one hundred Key Stage 1 and 2 trainees, no one had seen philosophical inquiry sessions or even heard this strategy being discussed.

Reflection

Perhaps you can think of some reasons why philosophy isn't a regular part of most school timetables.

How to fit a session of philosophical inquiry into a busy timetable is a tricky problem. Even trickier, you might say, is how to adapt this inquiry-based teaching for younger children. In Key Stage 2, children have learnt some of the skills required for philosophy: but what are those skills? As a trained philosopher, I offer you my checklist, which is a 'best fit' model.

Quickfall's philosopher checklist

You must have ideas
You should be playful (see Figure 2.2)
You ideally need to have opinions
You should be able to communicate your opinions
If at all possible, you should be prepared to listen to the ideas and opinions of others

Let me explain this very serious list. I have taught a lot of children, but never met one who wouldn't meet the criteria. Babies have ideas. My son, aged around eight months, had an idea that when I left the room I was still somewhere in the world – an idea about object permanence. This resulted in him having some very vocal opinions about me leaving the room, which he communicated clearly. As a toddler, he had ideas that involved climbing on precarious pieces of furniture, in a playful and creative way. Again, he had very strong opinions on this; although he did listen to my opinions, he put forward a forceful rebuttal to my argument. As a three-year-old, he has ideas and opinions and communicates in many ways. He confidently asks questions, such as whether Scotland is in fact made of dinosaur poo (when you think about it, some of it must be). He can think about his thinking: he can do meta-cognition, at three years of age. If I ask him how he came up with his latest cunning plan (making a 'rock parlour' – see see photographs below, Figures 2.3 and 2.4), he can reflect and then try to blame his dad for giving him the idea. He does not worry about being wrong, or saying something inappropriate

Figure 2.2 Having playful ideas
Photograph by Aimee Quickfall, 2017

(even in front of large crowds). His thinking is perhaps as free as it ever will be during his childhood. Typing those words makes me feel incredibly sad, but I think it might be true. There is evidence to suggest that by the time children have moved some way through the primary phase, the 'amount of time spent on creative teaching, investigation, play, practical work etc. has reduced considerably, and lessons more often have a standard format' (Hutchings, 2015, p.5). This is not the case for every child, or every school, but children learn very early in their lives that there are certain answers that are required, if they are to succeed. As a teacher commented, 'They are six years old, and all their school experience tells them is that they are failures' (Hutchings, 2015, p.33).

Making a 'rock parlour'

Ahh, but not in the early years, Aimee, you are thinking (maybe). That is why I am willing to bet my best hat that the Early Years Foundation Stage (EYFS) is our best hope for developing the creative thinkers that the world needs. In our settings and classrooms, I am sure you will have fond memories of the genius ideas that your young learners have

Figure 2.3 Making a rock parlour, part 1
Photograph by Aimee Quickfall, 2017

delighted you and each other with. In the early years we use play to learn, we hopefully discuss the surreal fantasy worlds of role play as easily as we discuss favourite pizza toppings, and with the same level of concentration and passion. Opinions are strenuously defended, and yet our children can change their views as quickly as the tide. As practitioners, we understand that communication happens in many ways, we value this and encourage discussion and questioning. The sort of philosophical inquiry used in the research by Gorard, Siddiqui and See (2017) would meet many of the themes of the EYFS Framework (Department for Education, 2014), in terms of valuing the unique child and creating an enabling environment, but also in specific areas of learning, where the verbal and non-verbal communication of a discussion, the turn taking, listening, respect for different views and sharing experiences and memories are valued.

I often reflect upon the idea that my philosophy lecturers at university had much in common with my Reception class. They were rewarded for being creative with their thinking, they discussed their ideas with friends and adversaries; they held opinions that were, at times, considered a little strange or unusual…but they were confident in their thoughts. They were toddlers with a very large vocabulary and slightly better table

Figure 2.4 Making a rock parlour, part 2
Photograph by Aimee Quickfall, 2017

manners (and sometimes mismatched shoes). So why couldn't our child philosophers be just as successful?

There are critics of philosophy with and for children, from a number of different traditions and 'schools of thought' – I am not going to discuss them all here, but a few of these are particularly relevant to the early years. If you are interested in reading further on the main critiques, there are some resources at the end of the chapter that will get you started.

The main opposition to using philosophical inquiry with young children comes from developmental stage theories of child development, notably Piaget's theory on the development of children through four distinct cognitive stages (Piaget, 1972). According to Piaget, it is only when children reach the 'Concrete Operational Stage' that they can work things out for themselves, in their heads, without experiments or physical apparatus. Usually, the beginning of this stage is associated with children between the ages of seven and eleven. If children do develop in predictable stages, then Piaget's model would suggest that philosophical abstract thinking isn't likely to occur before the age of seven, and therefore inquiry teaching and learning would be not just a waste of time, but also confusing and potentially distressing for the children, as they might be aware of the frustrations of their teachers and their own 'failure' on a task for which they are developmentally unprepared. Game over for philosophy in the early years, then, where Piaget might put most of the children in a 'pre-operational stage,' where egocentrism means that children cannot see from another person's point of view.

But hang on, the chapter clearly doesn't end for several more pages – the game is back on! Well, I think it is. Let me explain how we can neatly sidestep Piaget here. Now, I would not wish to suggest that there is no truth to stage theories of child development; they have been influential in education and childcare for over 100 years and can be helpful when trying to identify (or reassure) about developmentally appropriate behaviours and achievements. However, I think even Piaget would acknowledge some holes in the argument. For a start, Piaget was difficult to pin down on the ages that linked to stages, and subsequent research has even suggested that many adults (up to two thirds) never meet the formal operational stage, by Piaget's measurements (Dassen, 1994), which children are expected to have reached by the age of 11. This would suggest that most adults are not capable of philosophical inquiry either, which I don't think is true! Secondly, Piaget was a very tough assessor of ability – in fact, some critics have suggested that what he observed was not understanding, but performing; a toddler may not get up and hunt around for a hidden object, but that doesn't mean that they don't understand that it is still in the world. His experiments would be considered quite confusing by today's standards and it is likely that many children were done a disservice in his observations, as the tasks were inaccessible. From your own experiences of being with young children, have you ever known a child under seven years old who can appreciate the viewpoint of another person? Perhaps you have known children who help someone who is hurt, showing that they understand their pain and upset. Maybe you have spoken with young children who are concerned about Mummy or Daddy going to work, or who ask if you are cold when you have been on playground duty! My little boy has shown understanding of viewpoint in his small world play since he was around 18 months old (and potentially had this understanding much earlier without showing it/being recognised), worrying about toys left outside in a tent, because 'they cold now' (see Figure 2.5); other theorists have had similar experiences with young children (Donaldson, 1978; Lipman, 1998).

Rescuing toys from the cold tent

Another criticism of philosophical inquiry with children comes from some commentators who suggest that children are not equipped to 'do philosophy' (for example, Hayes, 2015). Again, this can be taken alongside the child development stages objection, but underlying this critique is the question of exactly what we mean when we talk about philosophical thinking. Some thinkers have objected to the idea that children could have meaningful philosophical thoughts, because they do not have the pre-requisite skills and

Figure 2.5 Rescuing toys from the cold tent
Photograph by Aimee Quickfall, 2017

knowledge to engage with the project. It is posited that without a broad foundation of experiences, it is impossible to reflect. A famous philosophical conundrum, the 'Ship of Theseus' paradox, has been given as an example (Murris, 2000) – very briefly, a ship is replaced, plank by plank, until none of the original components remain; is it still the same ship? If the replaced parts were all assembled to make another ship, which one would be the true Ship of Theseus? Murris (2000) uses this argument as part of a discussion on whether philosophy with young children is possible, supposing that the children might not have a clear understanding of the story at all, and perhaps would not have a concept of identity to support their thinking about this paradox.

Again, we can answer this critique with a nod to the presentation/understanding difficulty, highlighted in Piaget's studies. How can we know what children understand of these kinds of puzzle? Fricker (2007) calls this epistemic injustice – a 'moral wrongdoing to a person in their capacity as a knower' (p.17). Haynes and Murris (2013) put forward an argument for questioning our practice and interactions with children, to ensure that we do not talk down to them or sentimentalise their ideas. I know I have been guilty of this – especially when children are playing fantasy and magical games, adults may underestimate the thinking that underpins the play (Egan, 1988), and I know I have not taken enough time to observe and be involved in these learning events. Matthews (1995) suggests that the issue here is actually based on a sort of snobbery about what philosophical thought is and should be – after all, we do not shy away from teaching young children about numbers, just because they are not ready to tackle theoretical mathematics at degree level. He puts forward a similar rejection to that of Dassen (1994) when he asserts that, actually, many adults would struggle to think about paradoxes and philosophical questions in the same way a 'professional' philosopher would. You can also look at this from a postmodern perspective and question why the adult way of philosophising is considered better or higher – the 'stages of child development' models could be construed as suggesting that children's questioning, reasoning and reflection are somehow not as good; that they are not the finished article. Applying a developmental scale to thinking presumes a graduation from one stage to the next – each stage is an improvement rather than a change. Matthews (1995) would suggest that children have the approach to inquiry that philosophers work hard to relearn in adulthood. They have wonder, curiosity; they are unafraid of error; they ask the same big questions that are the very stuff of philosophy, as you will know if you have spent a few days with young children.

So if we accept that children are capable of philosophical inquiry, what is the real difference between our young learners and the academic philosophers, aside from the intake of caffeine and the private office space? Professional philosophers can expect to have the following experiences (I am told that in France, companies sometimes recruit company philosophers – what a fantastic title!)

What 'grown up' philosophers need

They have had the time and space to reflect, to wonder, to be curious.
They have had questions and comments from peers that have helped to shape their ideas.
They have engaged with great and seemingly unfathomable mysteries (see Figure 2.6).
Their ideas and theories have been noticed; recognition has been given.

These areas also need to be addressed for our young philosophers, and this is where we begin our philosophical teaching and learning in the early years.

Figure 2.6 Engaging with mysteries
Photograph by Aimee Quickfall, 2017

Time and space for thinking

Young children, like their professional counterparts, need spaces for thinking. For some adult philosophers, this means an office crammed with books, teacups and odd shoes (you know who you are!), but it could also be the trunk of a beautiful tree to lean upon, a favourite spot in a coffee shop or the strange oasis of calm that is sometimes achieved during a train journey into work. For our learners, variety of space and place is also required. Some children do their best thinking in a quiet place, others in a busy place. Some like to be outside (I have generally found opening the door to an outside area to be the easiest boost to thinking); some like to be in a cosy, enclosed space. If we do not provide those spaces, we cannot expect all of our philosophers to blossom in our settings. Children will show you (even if they cannot tell you) where they do their best thinking. It might be in a different place every day. Through your observations of play, you will know the spaces that work for your learners. What we often do not identify is the space we are not providing, the missing philosopher's office. Next time you are observing an EYFS setting, check for thinking spaces.

Thinking spaces checklist

Have we provided:

Quiet space for individuals and groups of children?
Enclosed, cosy spaces?
Areas for collaborative thinking outdoors and indoors?
Opportunities for learners to set up or build their own thinking dens?

Of course, every setting has to work with a limited budget, a sometimes labyrinth-like floor plan and a multitude of other constraints. What I can tell you is that if you create some of these spaces, you will find the benefits for yourself. A quiet space will allow children to concentrate on other activities, such as looking at books or listening with focus, as well as improving the opportunities for deeper thinking in your setting.

Time for thinking

I have definitely been guilty of the 'stop, start' model of early years – where the day is broken up by story time, snack time, phonics time…and those interruptions have an impact on learning and on children's feelings of control over their play. 'It is not uncommon to see adults unknowingly/unintentionally interrupting children's play with arguably inappropriate pedagogical acts' (Weldemariam, 2014). If we want to encourage the next generation of philosophers, we need to give their thinking time priority and proper respect.

It is not always a realistic goal to cut out these interruptions altogether; if you are preparing a Reception class for Key Stage 1, you might be taking them to assemblies, involving them in playtime with the older children and giving them more teaching inputs. However, it is worth considering how much sustained thinking time children have in your setting. It is easy to work this out, using your timetable or routine as a guide and then considering how often children are individually interrupted, perhaps by small group support sessions or one-to-one interventions (if you do these). For effective play and problem solving, children need sustained periods to be immersed in their ideas. I would suggest that a good goal is for children to have at least 45 minutes of uninter-rupted time every day in a 'free flow' environment, and longer if you can manage it. I have often been frustrated by the 'flightiness' of interactions with the provision in my settings, when children will spend a few seconds at each activity – but what can we expect, if we are constantly breaking their concentration to engage in potentially less interesting or rewarding activities? Simple solutions can help and visiting other settings sometimes brings these alternatives to light – for example, having a snack station where children can help themselves avoids breaking up the session. Planning whole group inputs for the beginning or the end of the session can also help to give the children 'a good run' at their playing, thinking and collaborating.

Independence and community

Thinking together may seem like a difficult prospect with very young children, but they are effective collaborative learners already. Babies and toddlers are superb at capitalising on the modelling that goes on around them. Young children are brilliant at learning from each other, as you will know if you have ever witnessed the speed at which a 'naughty word' is spread amongst a group. The difficulty here is knowing when to interact, intervene and interrupt, as the adult in the room. Research by Weldemariam (2014) would suggest that many adult interventions in play are the end of the thinking, so how can we approach philosophical inquiry with individual children and groups?

The model of inquiry used with older children tends to follow a rough pattern (see Cassidy and Christie, 2013; McCall, 2009). This list is based on my experiences of adapting philosophy-for/with-children models:

- There is a facilitator, adult or child, responsible for ensuring all have a chance to speak and that the discussion is focussed on the question.
- There is a sense of community; sessions begin with games that help to build the team.
- The process starts with a stimulus – perhaps a photograph, drawing, story, sound or song, a smell…anything that will provoke a response.
- Independent thinking comes next, when children have a chance to generate a word to describe the stimulus, on their own.
- Paired work follows: children share their word with a partner and explain why they chose it. If the children are ready, they may then come up with a question from their words.
- Words or questions are then studied by the group – are there connections to be made? Do some of the words/questions have the same meaning, or something else in common?
- There is a shared responsibility and democracy – the group vote for the word/ question they want to discuss.
- At this point, if the group have used individual words up to now, the facilitator may suggest questions relating to the words that would help to start a discussion.
- Children sit in a circle to discuss the word/question. The facilitator watches for children who have something to say and may respectfully interject to involve others.
- Final words – at the end of the discussion, each child is given the opportunity to summarise their thinking – this may be by showing whether they have changed their mind, or sharing something that they admired about someone else.

With older children (Key Stage 2, for example) the role of the adult in these sessions is absolutely minimal and I withdraw from the role of facilitator as quickly as I can; in my experience, within a few one-hour sessions I can have very little input and children run the community of inquiry themselves. I never give an opinion in these sessions – I try not to show a preference for any question or word, I might question the connections between their ideas but attempt to show no preference for one idea over another. With younger children, there is a temptation to increase the role of the adult in this community, but I think this is a mistake. Young children may need the adult to take a facilitator role for longer, purely because the nature of a 'free flow' environment makes gathering a large group of children on one activity quite tricky...although we do witness these big group projects, managed and organised by young children. A particular example that springs to mind is a watercourse that was created in my Reception outdoor area, by a team that included almost every child in the cohort at some point and resulted in the flooding of part of the garden when we left it set up over a stormy weekend! A genuine example of our young learners being capable of changing the world, as evidenced by a family of ducks (momentarily) deciding to set up a home there, and the look on my head teacher's face.

I am going to suggest a model for philosophical inquiry with young children, which I have used with different groups and individual children. This might be a completely new strategy for you, or it could be part of your practice that you have not considered as philosophical inquiry. You might find, after reading this, that you are already a fully paid-up philosophical inquiry facilitator, in which case, your next step might be to ensure your practice is shared and recognised.

The classic philosophical inquiry

Simple Model of Inquiry:

Stimulate
Explore
Connect
Question
Reconnect

STIMULATE: Working from the pattern used with older children, choose a stimulus to share with a group. Pictures work well, or objects that can be touched and handled (see Figure 2.7). Stories are also brilliant; if you haven't tried it before, tell a story from memory instead of a book.

Figure 2.7 Exploring and reflecting
Photograph by Aimee Quickfall, 2017

Some suggestions for stimuli:

- Empty snail or sea shells
- Cut flowers (fresh ones, or flowers that are past their best make a very interesting talking point)
- Photos of the children themselves, working together, concentrating, helping each other.
- Food (especially if you can let the children have a taste!)
- Special objects – blankets, toys, precious mementos.

EXPLORE: Ask children to touch, smell, listen and look at the stimulus. Collect their first thoughts about it: often these will be quite obvious to an adult, but young children might be exploring a concept for the first time at this point. When someone says 'empty' when exploring a snail shell, it opens up many lines of inquiry. Who lived there? What happened? Babies and toddlers can touch, smell and taste, even if they cannot verbalise their ideas. Their faces will tell a story for them; try holding up a mirror so they can see their own reaction, or take a photo that can be displayed with the stimulus to remind them of the sensation.

CONNECT: In my opinion, this is the most important part of any inquiry. Ask the children (if they have not started already) to think about their thinking: is their idea like anyone else's? Did some people say the same thing? With very young or non-verbal children, using a stimulus they can move around really helps. For simple like/dislike decisions, you can ask the children if they want to keep the object, or swap it for something else. This can easily be recorded in drawings, photos and brief notes that can be shared with parents and the children in later sessions.

This metacognition encourages the children to a deeper level of thinking (Samuelsson and Carlsson, 2008). It seems very simple, but noticing that your idea is a bit like that of someone else opens up a new world. There is a connection there, between two people, and the start of a friendship, but also there is a fascinating peep into the way someone else thinks and feels. Noticing how ideas can be different is equally valuable. This is the part of the inquiry that potentially has the most impact and takes the session beyond what we would do if we were aiming to broaden vocabulary, or share feelings about something…but it is often the activity which is missed out.

This may be enough for young children and I would encourage you to allow your philosophers to wander in and out of the discussion, rather than setting up a strict session with obligations to take part. You will probably find that they want to stay involved for a lot longer than they would in a more formal teacher input, based on my experiences.

QUESTION: The next stage is to begin questioning, based on their observations and ideas. For example, when exploring photographs of the children from several months previously, the group were amused and delighted by how much they had changed, and their words and ideas reflected this. They used words to describe their development since then; 'I'm much bigger now' and 'I can do that super speedy, I was slow.' My questioning was focussed on the differences from then to now, but quickly moved into what was still the same. It was a simple and short discussion, but in five minutes we had shared our hopes that our friends would always be with us, that we thought we would change again and look back at our current selves in a similar way, and that there are some things about us that don't change. In terms of philosophy, the children were hitting some of the big ideas around identity, just like that old Ship of Theseus; just by looking at photographs and being introduced to ways of thinking, by using some questions.

RECONNECT: Finally, it really helps to summarise the ideas that have been shared and discussed. This could be as simple as sharing the stimulus again, and sharing a word or two to describe it. For the adult involved, this is generally really interesting, as some children will stick with their original response, some will have come up with a new idea, some will have taken on board the ideas of others and adapted their own. You could keep a record of responses shared, which is a lovely thing to share with parents. Children could draw a picture to represent the session, or take the stimulus for use in their play.

It is possible to use this model with individual children, pairs or a larger group. Once you have tried it, you will find that there are natural opportunities for including philosophical inquiry in your inputs and interactions in play. The trick now is to know when it is appropriate to intervene in play to pursue the 'deeper' level of thinking. Sometimes children do not need an adult to facilitate deep thinking; moreover, play is an opportunity for so much more than philosophical inquiry.

The magic of a mystery

As well as using a rough model for philosophical inquiry, one aspect of the professional philosopher's life, which I don't think should be overlooked, is the fascination with a mystery. Philosophers might spend their whole life discussing one strand of philosophy – mathematics, science, mind, ethics; they might concentrate on one or two questions in these strands, over years of scholarship. They do this because they are fascinated. Something about that area of philosophy has captivated them; there is a mystery that they must explore. Children exemplify this behaviour and quest, as they can also be completely captivated by a mystery, in ways that the average adult probably doesn't have the time, energy or focus to achieve. Obviously, dear reader, I am not including you in that bracket, as you have got this far into the chapter and are clearly a highly discerning reader.

Bringing mystery and intrigue into your setting will encourage the questioning and wondering that makes a super philosopher. It will also make you incredibly popular. Mysteries don't need to be expensive or elaborate; in fact, I think they are more effective when they are cheap and simple. I have got a few tried and tested examples, but you will think of many more for yourself – part of the skill with this is timing and frequency. If you have a new mystery every day, it could be exhausting or boring. If you spring a mystery on the children when they are already feeling disrupted by a change to the timetable or staff, the mystery could just be another traumatic event. Trust your knowledge and understanding of the children and even if you have got a magnificent mystery planned, if the timing isn't right, save it for another day.

The 'where on Earth?' mystery

This mystery is a big game of hide and seek. I have a favourite puppet, Sid, who helps me with phonics and gets up to mischief (he always gets the blame when phonics cards go missing). One very memorable mystery was when Sid went missing himself, which wasn't planned as a mystery at all! The children noticed that Sid wasn't on my chair as usual, so all of the 'setting up' part of the mystery was done by them, questioning each other and trying to remember who had seen him. In fact, Sid had gone home to be washed, but the mystery was too delightful to abandon. Sid left some clues, over the following few days, suggesting that he might have gone somewhere on his own, without telling his parents or friends (a bit of Personal, Social and Emotional Development, sneaking in). The children used their free flow time to make posters, rescue equipment including ladders and life rafts and to search for Sid. Sid was found, safe and well, stuck in a pile of tyres in the garden. Phew! This fed naturally into discussions about what had happened and what Sid could do next time to stay safe. He got many a stern 'talking to' about being more careful.

The 'what's in the box?' mystery

This is a classic and I can't take any credit for it, as you have probably used it yourself in various ways. Basically, there is a container which contains a mystery object – the tension and excitement builds until the mysterious item is revealed. It might be a beautifully wrapped present that is opened, or a treasure chest, or a bag…Usually, this is an anticlimax, as the children have imagined wonderful and amazing contents that you can't possibly live up to. There are a few ways to make your 'reveal' more exciting, including changing the rest of the environment, for example, making the room darker than usual or playing some exciting drum roll music. If you have asked the children to guess what is inside, and given clues, they have probably come pretty close to the contents and the surprise is exciting because it is validating. Trying a mysterious object such as a mirror or photographs of the children can be really effective at demonstrating how special and valued they are.

The 'what happens next?' mystery

This is another classic – I am sure you have used this with stories, asking someone to predict what happens next, before continuing. As with the mystery box, children will often come up with very interesting and exciting ideas for the ending of stories. Using film clips and animation can add to this mystery, particularly if you can involve people they know – a well-loved cartoon character will have more impact, so imagine the connection they feel to a film when it stars you, or their lunchtime supervisor, or the librarian. Now, if you put that person in a situation involving 'mild peril' – perhaps they are locked out of the house, or are about to step into a really stinky dog poo – the level of involvement from your young philosophers is increased many fold. Especially if there is poo involved.

This mystery technique can also lend itself well to experimentation. It does not have to be one of the traditional classroom experiments, such as what happens to an egg when cooked (I would be very surprised to hear of any child that carried out that experiment without knowing the answer – not much mystery involved). It could be a mystery that you do not know the answer to, either. A good one is what happens if you mix lemonade, cooking oil and food colouring. I do not want to spoil it for you, but the results vary depending on order and quantity – but the predictions you will get before you start mixing are fantastic. The wilder the better, I think; who is to say that this combination could not generate leopard-print unicorns? Well, certainly I am in no position to rule it out. The children are given a message here – that experimentation is exciting – and that sometimes adults do not know the answers either, so mysteries and discoveries are possible, even if you are as old and wise as Miss Q.

Noticing and celebrating the philosophy

This is the easiest bit – but also the hardest, as happens so often in philosophy. Just when you think you have understood something, another layer begins to reveal itself, even deeper and more complex than the last. The easy/hard thing is noticing when philosophical inquiry is taking place in your setting, so that you can maximise the potential, encourage and celebrate it. My advice on noticing the philosophy in the early years is to train everyone around you to notice it, praise it, reward it and celebrate it. If all your young learners know how to spot a good idea, then also know that a way to keep good ideas going is to be excited about them, your work will be done (at least partially!) for you. I knew I was on the right track with my first Reception class when I overheard a couple of dinosaur boys (you know them – children who can, and will, tell you everything there is to know about dinosaurs. They can read 'Tyrannosaurus Rex,' even though they haven't done a single session of synthetic phonics yet), congratulating a classmate on the amazing idea they had just explained. What made me even more proud was that the idea did not have anything to do with prehistoric reptiles, but the boys could still recognise how interesting and exciting it was.

In terms of celebrating the philosophy, as with all things, please yourselves...some people like stickers, some like to have a prize box or a special celebration dance! I do think the world would be a better place if instead of the usual awards, we gave certificates for the best idea of the week, or the most interesting answer to a question. Now imagine how powerful that would be if the children nominated the winners. It might sound like a lot to ask of our youngest learners, but if we don't ask those questions, we will never find out whether they can answer them. If you don't believe me, try asking a three-year-old who comes up with the best games at preschool, or who has the most exciting plans. If you ask in the right way, they will tell you. If they can't verbalise these ideas, observe them; their play will tell you.

You could make a display to share your ideas with the rest of the school, invite parents and carers in to take part in inquiry sessions (this isn't as scary as it sounds, and grandparents are often really keen to come in and share a mystery); you could make philosophical inquiry part of your plan for transition into the next setting or class.

Celebrating the thinking

Some ideas:

Make a philosophical inquiry display, using the records you make with the children of their ideas.

Involve parents and carers in your inquiries – pose philosophical questions on notice boards or using social media. Even better if you can use questions the children have asked.

Share the thinking you have observed with parents through learning journals.

Celebrate good ideas and creative thinking; perhaps with a simple certificate to take home.

The whole world needs to know about your philosophical inquiry; because philosophy doesn't live unless you breathe it on everyone!

Further reading on philosophy with/for children

These are articles that I have found particularly clear and useful; there are many books and some journals dedicated to this area so you won't run out of bedtime reading!

What is it all about?

Cassidy, C. & Christie, D. (2013). Philosophy with children: talking, thinking and learning together. *Early Child Development and Care*, 183:8, 1072–1083.

Haynes, J. & Murris, K. (2013). The realm of meaning: imagination, narrative and playfulness in philosophical exploration with young children. *Early Child Development and Care*, 183:8, 1084–1100.

McCall, C. (2009). *Transforming Thinking: Philosophical Inquiry in the Primary and Secondary Classroom*. London: Routledge.

Pohoata, G. & Petrescu, C. 2013). Is there a philosophy for children? *Euromentor Journal*, 5:3.

Vasieleghem, N. & Kennedy, D. (2011). What is a philosophy for children, what is philosophy with children – after Matthew Lipman? *Journal of Philosophy of Education*, 45:2.

The arguments for, against and respectfully sceptical

Gregory, M. (2011). Philosophy for children and its critics: A Mendham dialogue. *Journal of Philosophy of Education*, 45:2.

Trickey, S. & Topping, K.J. (2004). 'Philosophy for children': a systematic review. *Research Papers in Education*, 19:3, 365–380.

Recent research studies

Education Endowment Foundation (2015). *Philosophy for children evaluation report and executive summary*, July 2015. Independent evaluators: Stephen Gorard. Nadia Siddiqui and BengHuat See (Durham University) https:// educationendowmentfoundation.org.uk/uploads/pdf/Philosophy_for_Children. pdf

Gorard, S., Siddiqui, N. and See, B.H. (2017). Can 'philosophy for children' improve primary school attainment? *Journal of Philosophy of Education*, http://onlinelibrary.wiley.com/doi/10.1111/1467–9752.12227/abstract

Siddiqui, N. and Gorard, S. and See, B.H. (2017). *'Non-cognitive impacts of philosophy for children.'* Project Report. School of Education, Durham University, Durham

References

Cassidy, C. and Christie, D. (2013). Philosophy with children: talking, thinking and learning together. *Early Child Development and Care*, 183:8, 1072–1083.

Dassen, P. (1994). Culture and cognitive development from a Piagetian perspective. In W. J. Lonner and R.S. Malpass (Eds.), *Psychology and Culture*. Boston: Allyn and Bacon.

Department for Education (2014). *Statutory Framework for the Early Years Foundation Stage: setting the standards for learning, development and care for children from birth to five.* https://www.gov.uk/government/publications/early-years-foundation-stage-framework–2.

Donaldson, M. (1978). *Children's Minds*. London: Fontana.

Education Endowment Foundation (2015). *Philosophy for children evaluation report and executive summary, July 2015*. Independent evaluators: Stephen Gorard. Nadia Siddiqui and Beng Huat See (Durham University) Accessed 15.07.15. https:// educationendowmentfoundation.org.uk/uploads/pdf/Philosophy_for_Children. pdf

Egan, K. (1988). *Primary Understanding: Education in Early Childhood*. Abingdon: Routledge.

Fricker, M. (2007). *Epistemic Injustice: Power and the Ethics of Knowing*. Oxford: Oxford University Press.

Gorard, S., Siddiqui, N. and See, BH (2017) Can 'Philosophy for Children' improve primary school attainment? *Journal of Philosophy of Education*, http://onlinelibrary.wiley.com/doi/10.1111/1467–9752.12227/abstract

Gregory, M. (2011). Philosophy for children and its critics: A mendham dialogue. *Journal of Philosophy of Education*, 45:2.

Hayes, D. (2015) Philosophy for Children isn't Real Philosophy. Available at: http://www.spiked-online.com/newsite/article/philosophy-for-children-isnt-real-philosophy/17193#.V63HQ1srJpg (Last seen on 12th August 2016)

Haynes, J. and Murris, K. (2013). The realm of meaning: imagination, narrative and playfulness in philosophical exploration with young children. *Early Child Development and Care*, 183:8, 1084–1100.

Hutchings, M. (2015). *Exam factories? The impact of accountability measures on children and young people*. London: National Union of Teachers.

Lacey, A.R. (1976). *A Dictionary of Philosophy*. Abingdon: Routledge & Kegan Paul.

Lipman, M. (1998). Teaching students to think reasonably: Some findings of the philosophy for children program. *The Clearing House: A Journal of Educational Strategies, Issues and Ideas*, 71:5, 277–280.

Matthews, G. (1995). *The Philosophy of Childhood*. Cambridge, MA: Harvard University Press.

McCall, C. (2009). *Transforming Thinking: Philosophical Inquiry in the Primary and Secondary Classroom*. Abingdon: Routledge.

Murris, K. (2000). Can children do philosophy? *Journal of Philosophy of Education*, 34:2.

Piaget, J. (1972). *The Psychology of the Child*. New York: Basic Books.

Pohoata, G. and Petrescu, C. 2013). Is there a philosophy for children? *Euromentor Journal*, 5:3.

Samuelsson, I. and Carlsson, M. (2008). The playing learning child: towards a pedagogy of early childhood. *Scandinavian Journal of Educational Research*, 53:6.

Siddiqui, N., Gorard, S. and See, B.H. (2017) '*Non-cognitive impacts of philosophy for children.,*' Project Report. Durham: School of Education, Durham University.

Trickey, S. and Topping, K.J. (2004). 'Philosophy for children': a systematic review. *Research Papers in Education*, 19:3, 365–380.

Vasieleghem, N. and Kennedy, D. (2011). What is a philosophy for children, what is philosophy with whildren – after Matthew Lipman? *Journal of Philosophy of Education*, 45:2.

Weldemariam, K. (2014). Cautionary tales on interrupting children's play: a study from Sweden. *Childhood Education*, 90:4.

Thinking about leadership in the early years sector

Jonathan Wainwright

Overview

This chapter explores the complexities of leadership and gives insights into how effective leadership manifests itself in the early years. Key theorists are discussed and ways of developing authentic leadership considered.

> The idea of leadership is complex, difficult to capture and open to numerous definitions and interpretations. Neither in common parlance nor in the literature on the subject is there consensus about the essences of leadership, or the means by which it can be identified, achieved or measured. Although it is spoken about as a concrete and observable phenomenon, it remains an intangible illusive notion, no more stable than quicksand.
>
> (Middlehurst, 1993)

I hope that it will not seem too strange to have a chapter on leadership in a book on putting philosophy into practice. My argument about its inclusion is that it is a subject that has fascinated many people for a long time and has been the subject of a huge number of books and papers. We only have to look at recent political events to see how much it features in news headlines and the conversations of the day.

Typing the word 'leadership' into Google (August 2017) gives 832 million hits – a similar search gives the Kardashians 62 million and Ed Sheeran a mere 52 million. Whilst I would never dismiss the popularity of celebrity, it seems as though the complex idea of leadership is of even greater popular interest.

This chapter seeks to say something about the reasons behind the importance of leadership and why there is so much interest in the idea. It will focus on the idea of authentic leadership and its relevance for early years settings, and suggest a way of exploring our personal philosophies of leadership and how we might put those into practice.

However, as we proceed through the chapter please keep in mind Middlehurst's (1993) words above – leadership 'remains an *'illusive notion.'*

Reflections

Write down the names of five people you know who you would see as leaders.
What makes you want to follow them?
Where do we start?

The reflection point above is clearly underpinned by an assumption that leadership lies within individual leaders – in fact, this is how studies of leadership have emerged with a focus on the 'Great Man,' as first expressed by Thomas Carlyle in 1904.

Case et al. (2011) say that the noun 'leader' first appeared around 1300. The concept of leading had existed before then, in terms of say kings and queens, and the word is said to originate from and old word *Loedan*, meaning to 'cause someone to go with oneself'; it 'describes the way in which we human beings will show one another the way – and allow ourselves to be shown or guided' (Case et al., 2011, p.5). This seems a gentler expression than some of the 20th-century approaches, particularly more instrumental approaches where the purpose of leadership was seen as purely to deliver organisational (and usually business) objectives. This put leadership outside of any moral stance – exemplified by Milton Friedman's (1970) view that the only social responsibility of business is to make a profit.

I think that this view is at odds with how we see the focus of what we do in our sector – and increasingly in many others. In many ways, we adopt a completely opposite perspective, one which I think we would see as being more governed by morality and ethics. Though we do function as 'businesses,' in that organisations have to survive in order to be able to achieve their goals, our work is purely about social responsibility and I feel that we would at least try to put children before cuts, ethics over efficiency, pedagogy before profit and staff before shareholders.

Before exploring issues around the leadership approach which I think can support us in achieving these things, it is useful to explore the development of leadership thinking so that we can develop a more informed perspective on what might work for us.

Leadership: an introduction

Historical approaches to studying leadership (which have usually been in business) examine the field from a number of perspectives, notably trait theory, skills theory, behavioural theory and situational theory (see Northouse, 2016 for an excellent account of the various theories about leadership). Studies in the field of early years leadership has basically followed the pattern of these studies of business leadership, though over a much shorter period of time.

Dunlop (2008) suggests that traditionally, research into leadership in the early years has been associated with the leader as a person, echoing the 'Great Man' idea we looked at earlier. It is important to note at this point that leadership study in the past has focussed predominantly on men as leaders. As we know, men make up only a very small percentage of staff in our sector, so we would have to question whether a different approach is necessary.

Research into our sector, again following the process adopted by business-based research, has focussed on the traits of the leader herself. These have been identified as including warmth, gentleness, enthusiasm, passion, inspiration and advocacy (Solly, 2003), caring (Osgood, 2006) and love (Dalli, 2005). Janet Moyles (2004) adds being visionary, flexible and charismatic and Aubrey (2007) adds rationality, knowledgeability and assertiveness. Aubrey (ibid.) suggests that the traits of being warm, nurturing and sympathetic may be a 'distinctive feature of early years providers and of female workers.' (p. 31).

Reflections

What do you think are the most important traits for an early years leader?
Which of the traits identified do you see in the leaders you chose earlier?
Do you see these traits as gendered?
Do you think they would work in every situation?

The problem with trait theory is that there is no definitive list of traits. It is also very hard to assess the impact of each individual trait on people or settings (De Rue et al., 2011) and, as you reflected on above, not all traits are transferable to other contexts.

Another way to look at leadership is by examining the skills or competencies of leaders. These are different from traits since they are rather more about doing than being. Moyles (2004) suggests that the important skills are management skills, such as planning and decision making, and personal skills, such as time management and communication.

Rodd (2013) suggests that early childhood leaders need skills which are related to team work, motivation, support, role definition and goal setting. Scrivens (2002) sees building relationships, shared decision-making and empowerment of others as important characteristics of good leadership in early years and Kagan and Hallmark (2001) add the ideas of political awareness, interpersonal communication skills, group facilitation skills (mostly conducting effective meetings), decision-making skills (particularly participative management) and staff development skills. Not too much to ask there, then.

Reflections

Consider the leadership skills in the list below:
Can you identify instances where you have used these skills or seen them used successfully?

- Planning
- Decision making
- Time management
- Communication
- Motivation
- Support
- Goal setting
- Building relationships
- Empowerment of others
- Political awareness
- Group facilitation skills

Staff development skills

When you were thinking about these skills, you might have considered that, once more, they are hard to define clearly – and indeed sometimes rather hard to distinguish from traits. Indeed, as with any leadership model there are criticisms. Northouse (2016) suggests that the skills often identified are not specific to leadership. Again, it is difficult to link skills to outcomes for children or settings. Many organisations still use competence-based approaches to assessing leadership. Though this can be useful in development, in my view, such an approach does not consider the whole person.

Writing about leadership then moved towards considering leadership as a set of behaviours or styles where familiar concepts like 'authoritative' (do as I tell you), 'laissez-faire' (do what you like) and 'democratic' (let's agree what to do together) leadership styles were inevitably seen to have different effects on teams.

Reflections

Think of examples of types of leadership.
Which work best for you – as a leader, as a follower?
Does the approach work in all circumstances?

The thinking about styles developed into ideas around transformational leadership (Burns, 1978; Bass, 1990; Jackson and Parry, 2008). I would argue too that current educational thinking around distributed leadership is within the 'leadership style' school of thought, since someone (i.e. the leader) is doing the distributing. The outcome of that distribution could then be seen as the product of a particular style. Sharp et al. (2012) give an example of a children's centre leader who has a distributed leadership style 'where staff take responsibility for key areas' (p. 51).

If traits, skills and styles can be rather challenging to pin down, the idea of leadership behaviours perhaps promises us something that we can actually observe. Leadership behaviours that are effective in the early years sector have been identified by Sharp et al (2012, p. 9) as follows:

- Using evidence to drive improvements in outcomes
- Using business skills strategically
- Facilitating open communication
- Embracing integrated working
- Motivating and empowering staff
- Being committed to their own learning and development

These tend to mirror those behaviours identified in more generic literature around building a vision, communicating effectively, managing relationships and managing the task.

Sharp et al (2012) suggests that these behaviours are underpinned by the skills of change management and by emotional intelligence traits. One might comment, then, that there is nothing to distinguish the business literature on leadership behaviour from that of the ECEC field. Conceptually this suggests that a leader in the sector may not need any specific experience.

Reflections

How important do you think it is that ECEC leaders should have specific experience of working with young children?

As an aside, I think that it is interesting to note that school academy chains seem increasingly to have people with business backgrounds as chief executives and have school principals reporting to them. Indeed, there is no longer a requirement for head teachers either to have a teaching qualification or to have been awarded the NPQH (National Professional Qualification for Headship).

In criticising style theory, Northouse (2016) suggests that this view of leadership does not link what leaders do with the outcomes of their behaviour. Further criticism of style theory comes from Antonakis et al. (2004) who suggest that the contribution of leaders' behaviour to success is also contingent on contextual factors. In other words, some behaviours work in some situations but not in others. Though hardly rocket science, as anyone working with children will know, this is a very important consideration in terms of understanding the thinking behind leadership.

From this brief look at theory, it seems clear that there are several elements central to our understanding of leadership: traits, behaviours and context. In addition to this, from various definitions of leadership, ideas of process, power (or influence) and goals can also be extrapolated. These elements have significant implications for this study.

If we define leadership as a process, it means we need to look at it as something that is not a trait of the leader herself, but rather as something that happens between the leader and the follower and is therefore not necessarily formally designated. Influencing others requires power, which can come from many sources – for instance the ability to reward or sanction followers, referent power (followers' identification with the leader), expertise or her position in the hierarchy (French and Raven, 1959). Consideration of the implications of power and the attainment of goals brings us back to the need to consider ethical questions in our thinking about leadership.

If there is, and I believe it to be so, a socially responsible element to our work we perhaps need to consider the idea of good leadership. Our philosophical approach to leadership lies in the discussion of whether leadership is good or bad (Case et al., 2011), which takes us away from perhaps less sophisticated thinking about leadership as simply getting things done through others.

Reflections

How would you define good and bad leadership?
What is influencing your thinking?
What is your ethical standpoint – what would you do/not do and in what circumstances?

Towards a greater understanding

Having had a brief look at some history, we need now to start drawing some ideas together. I think that Grint (2010) succinctly captures all the elements we have considered via four overarching questions, which help the process of thinking about leadership:

- Is it where 'leaders' operate that makes them leaders? (Leadership as position)
- Is it who 'leaders' are that makes them leaders? (Leadership as person)
- Is it what 'leaders' achieve that makes them leaders? (Leadership as results)
- Is it how 'leaders' get things done that makes them leaders? (Leadership as process)

Reflections

Consider Grint's questions above:
How would you answer them and what examples could you give to support your thinking?

These are very important questions – *Where* suggests that context, culture and perhaps hierarchy are significant. *Who* implies personality, bringing in traits and the idea of personal values and consequently the stories and experiences that make that person who they are. *What* suggests outcomes and *How* reintroduces us to ideas of relationships, good and bad leadership and the ethical and moral dimensions involved.

In the early years sector, much recent work has focused on models that emphasise the importance of relationships (for instance Jones and Pound (2008), Robins and Callan (2008) and Moyles (2004)), where the focus of accounts of leadership is on pedagogy, emotional literacy, team and community development, multi-agency working and leading in times of change. Leeson et al. (2012) argue that the models that help to theorise this thinking are relatively new and are transformational in nature. McDowall Clark and Murray (2012) and Briggs and Briggs (2009) also argue for new paradigms.

Briggs and Briggs' (2009) new paradigm involves:

- Self-awareness: in terms of the Johari window used to reveal the '*facade*' behind which leaders might hide their ineffectiveness.
- Ethical and authentic leadership: in terms of social responsibility, fairness and wellbeing.
- Community leadership: delivering services within the local area through partnerships – and developing social capital.
- Charismatic leadership.
- Leadership of place.

Though Briggs and Briggs' (2009) paradigm is basically a repackaging of ideas we have already explored, they do make two very significant points. Firstly, they say that, even

Table 3.1 Aspects of McDowall, Clark and Murray's new leadership paradigm

Catalytic agency	Reflective integrity	Relational interdependence
Passionate care	Value-based reflection	Developing a community
Self-belief	Consistency and	Leading partnerships
Sustaining impetus	competency	Making it happen
Encouraging others	Multiple knowledge	Valuing others
	Emotional engagement	
	Making a difference	

though we are moving away from the notion of heroic (trait theory) leadership, some of the original underpinning ideas still have significance for our understanding.

Secondly, they say, as we have considered earlier, that:

> Perhaps the most damning criticism is that the research supporting these new paradigms is that it is [sic] men who have studied other men to formulate these approaches, and to compound matters, the research has been predominantly undertaken in white dominated societies.
>
> (Briggs and Briggs, 2009, p. 50)

While this may be the case in the business world, it is good to know that as the amount of research in the early years increases, more and more participants in the studies tend to be female – though the research still mostly seems to be located in largely white societies.

McDowall Clark and Murray's (2012) new paradigm features three aspects, 'catalytic agency, reflective integrity and relational interdependence' (p.41), summarized in Table 3.1 below.

These complex terms reflect a view that constructions of leadership change to fit changing circumstances. In McDowall Clark and Murray's view, the idea of a hierarchical leader limits our understanding; by seeing leadership instead as a process we shift our focus away from formal authority and onto collaborative action. This is a move towards seeing leadership as systemic, i.e. as something linked and pervasive, which mirrors current thinking about school leadership.

Catalytic agency is defined as a willingness to take action and an inner recognition that a practitioner can make a difference; 'Reflective integrity suggests that leaders need to reflect on practice to prompt learning and understanding; integrity is seen to be both organisational and individual and ensures alignment and synergy between mission, vision and policy in order to create a shared, ethical purpose.' Relational interdependence is summed up as 'the connectivity in (our) actions and interactions – the recognition that, in order to be effective, we need each other' (McDowall Clark and Murray, 2012, p. 39).

Again, we might argue that this approach again seems to package previous ideas in new ways and this can be seen in the detail of the model when the authors break their themes down into attributes and behaviours (See McDowall Clark and Murray's (2012) interesting book).

However, as a model, it encompasses the leader as a person (and therefore has relevance to gender), her followers and the context in which leadership takes place. It also attempts to answer Grint's (2010) questions that we looked at earlier.

An authentic approach

In developing our thinking about leadership in the sector, I find that the idea of authentic leadership is one of the most helpful. Once again, we have to be wary of the emperor's new clothes, however, though Avolio et al. (2005) suggest that the concept of authentic leadership is 'perhaps the oldest, oldest, oldest wine in the traditional leadership bottle....' They emphasise its importance by saying that it 'is such a root construct that transcends other theories and helps to inform them in terms of what is and is not "genuinely" good leadership' (p. xxiii).

I find this particularly useful in our sector because of the introduction of the idea of 'good' leadership, again playing into our consideration of the importance of ethics and the nature of the work in our sector.

Avolio et al. (ibid) assert that authentic leadership can incorporate transformational, charismatic, servant, spiritual or other forms of leadership. However, in contrast to transformational leadership in particular, authentic leadership 'may or may not be charismatic' (p.329). Exact definitions vary but all place some emphasis on intrapersonal, developmental and interpersonal perspectives (Northouse, 2016).

It is perhaps helpful to look at three reasonably contemporary definitions of authentic leadership (Gardner et al., 2011).

First, Leeson et al. (2012) suggest that the idea of authentic leadership has 'become attractive to those concerned that other models do not effectively support leaders as they attempt to guide their settings and communities through tough, ever changing times' (p. 229). Authentic leaders are true to themselves and engender trust from others. Because they are trusted, they are followed and this motivates others. 'As people develop as authentic leaders, they are more concerned about serving others than they are about their own success or recognition' (George and Sims, 2007, p. xxxi). Interestingly, this reflects some of the ideas of servant leadership (Greenleaf, 1970), where the argument was made that good leaders focus on the needs of others and value everyone's involvement in community life. Greenleaf (1970) puts emphasis on the unconditional acceptance of others and the removal of social injustice.

Second, for Walumbwa et al. (2008) authentic leadership is a pattern of behaviour that focuses on creating a positive ethical climate, which leads to greater 'self-awareness, an internalized moral perspective, balanced processing of information, and relational transparency on the part of leaders working with followers, fostering positive self-development' (p. 94).

Third, for Whitehead (2009) an authentic leader is one who

> (1) is self-aware, humble, always seeking improvement, aware of those being led and looks out for the welfare of others; (2) fosters high degrees of trust by building an ethical and moral framework; and (3) is committed to organizational success within the construct of social values.
>
> (Whitehead, 2009, p. 850)

Of course, there is criticism of authentic leadership as a concept. Booker (2012) suggests that there is no clear definition and that, in itself, the concept does not imply moral integrity. Northouse (2016) meanwhile suggests that because the research is in its infancy, there is not as yet enough empirical evidence to give it validity. Northouse also states that the moral component assumed by many for this notion is not fully explained. He asks, for instance, how leaders' values are related to self-awareness, and again points out the Achilles' heel of so many leadership theories, i.e. how this approach links to outcomes. He asks how an authentic leader who is disorganised and lacking in technical competence can be an effective leader (p. 223–4).

Gardiner (2011) offers deeper objections; she argues that the theory is an example of privilege arising from an 'intrinsic belief in self-worth' and therefore fails to take into account the 'complexities related to gender and power' (p. 99). She also suggests that self-understanding might also lead to a case of mistaken identity.

Despite these criticisms, the concept of authentic leadership is a useful model for us in the ECEC sector for a number of reasons. First, it describes an approach to leadership which is 'transparent, morally grounded and responsive to the needs and values of others' (Northouse, 2016 p. 282). It is a type of leadership that is developed over time, as a lifelong learning process (Luthans and Avolio, 2003). Second, it is useful because it is shaped by life events that act as 'triggers to growth and greater authenticity' (Northouse, 2016, p. 270).

Reflections

How does the concept of authentic leadership compare with some of the other theories we have explored?

How might it, or not, be good fit with your understanding of the purpose of leadership in the ECEC sector?

Putting authentic leadership into practice

If we accept that authentic leadership is a useful model, then we need to think about how it is applicable to our work and, first, what it means to be authentic.

One of the key criteria for authentic leadership is the idea of self-awareness. I always think this is a problematic area – our own perception of ourselves does not necessarily correspond with the way in which others see us – however, if we have that knowledge, then it does make it easier to develop transparency. The Johari window is a useful illustration of this – the aim being to make the hidden and opaque areas larger. The Johari window is a model developed by Luft and Ingham (1955) which consists of four quadrants: open, façade, unknown and blind spot. The façade represents information that the subject is aware of, but their peers are not. The Johari window consists of four panes, known by various titles, but in this case I will use the terms below:

The open area: what we know about ourselves and what others know about us.
The façade: what we know but do not share, or how we present ourselves when we do not want people to see the real us.
The blind self: where others are aware of things about us that we do not know.
The unknown: where we and others are unaware of things about us.

Of course, in our personal lives the façade may – or may not – play a greater part, however in a leadership context, where relational transparency is helpful, perhaps we should look to expand the open area so that our leadership approach becomes more overt and therefore consistent. In order to do this we need to use a combination of telling others about ourselves, asking others for feedback and continually seeking to discover and learn. This will help us develop our relationships with others.

A representation is given in Figure 3.1, adapted from the model of Luft and Ingham (1955).

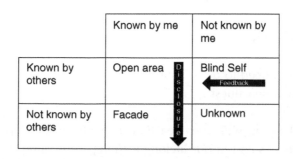

Figure 3.1 The Johari Window
Adapted from Luft and Ingham (1955)

▨ Activity

Have a go at drawing your own Johari window, focusing on yourself as a leader or potential leader. I think this is actually very difficult to do, but you might make a few attempts.

What could you disclose more clearly about yourself so that others better understand why you make the decisions that you do?

Think about what feedback would be useful to develop your leadership and understanding of that leadership. Think also about who you would like to get that feedback from.

Think about areas that you could explore or projects that you could undertake with others in order to learn more about yourself and your colleagues.

In order to avoid a case of mistaken identity, as Gardiner (2011) warns, it is worth exploring what our values are that underpin our own leadership philosophy. Peter Senge's (1994) list is helpful and he suggests that we undertake the following exercise:

1. Consider the list of 'values' (Table 3.2). Tick the ten which are the most important to you in the context of your life at work and outside of work – but also add more if you think that something important to you has not been included.
2. Now eliminate five of these top ten. Which would you give up if you had to? Cross them off: now imagine you are only allowed four. Which one would you give up? Cross it off.

   Now cross off another, to bring your list down to three. And another to bring it to two.

   Finally, cross off one of your two values.

   Which is the one item on the list that you care most about in the context of yourself, now and in a few years from now?
3. Take a look at the top three values on your list.

   a) What do they mean exactly? What are you expecting from yourself – even in bad times?
   b) How would your life be different if those values were more prominent and practised?
   c) What do you need to do in your life and leadership work to help you to stick strongly to those values?

Of course, in keeping with the idea that authentic leadership is something that develops over time – as part of our lifelong learning – our values do not also develop overnight, so it is worth considering our own journeys. Dalton and Dunnett (1992) suggest that major influences are as follows:

Table 3.2 Senge's list of values

Achievement	Friendship	Physical challenge
Advancement and promotion	Growth	Pleasure
Adventure	Having a family	Power and authority
Affection (love and caring)	Helping other people	Privacy
Arts	Helping society	Public service
Challenging problems	Independence	Publicity
Change and variety	Influencing others	Quality of work
Close relationships	Inner harmony	Quality of relationships
Community	Integrity	Recognition (respect)
Competence	Intellectual status	Religion
Competition	Involvement	Reputation
Co-operation	Job tranquillity	Responsibility
Creativity	Knowledge	Security
Decisiveness	Leadership	Self-respect
Democracy	Loyalty	Serenity
Ecological awareness	Meaningful work	Stability
Economic security	Merit	Status
Efficiency	Nature	Truth
Ethical practice	Personal development	Work with honest people

From Senge (1994)

Heredity: it's in the genes, family, race, class: I was born into it;
Others' influence: it was my friends;
External happenings: the critical incident;
Self-creation: I made up my mind.

Each of these has two possible responses. Heredity makes me how I am, but what can I make of it? Family gave me a path, but there are other roads. Others' influence shaped me, but I can be different. External happenings may mark the point either where I stopped, or where I took off. Self-creation asks us to think about making up our minds – I am myself, but what shall I become? Though this chapter is not intended to be therapeutic, if we are intending to be authentic in our leadership then these are things that we need to think about.

An example of this comes from Sam, who before she became a children's centre leader had been an emergency nurse. Describing how that work has helped her to become a good leader, Sam notes that part of her approach is about helping people not to dwell on situations, to learn from events and to move on. She worked with surgeons whose approach was to say 'You're either going to get much worse in 12 hours or you're going to get better – then it's move on to the next patient' (research interview with Wainwright). Sam says that she has adopted this kind of approach to her work:

> Something happens, reflect on it then move on quickly. I think I've always seen it as the fact that I'm able to move on with optimism and I drive people mad because things can happen and I just think there's no point dwelling on it.'
>
> (Jonathan Wainwright, research interview)

Another example comes from Margaret, who was a primary teacher before taking an ECEC leadership role. She says that people are amazed at how much time she spends on her work:

> Despite the fact that everybody sniggers and says you work from 9 till 3, we all know that we don't, so it's always been in my work ethic to work as long as I need to get the work done.
>
> (Jonathan Wainwright, research interview)

Saima describes how she was never a follower but always a leader:

> I think some of that relates to probably having children quite young and being on my own and having to have control and having to sort everything out for myself from quite a young age that I'm probably used to doing that taking over role. For me it's hard because I think I can be quite controlling.
>
> (Jonathan Wainwright, research interview)

Of course, these are very neat examples – but we can see how life stories are helpful in reflecting on leadership.

Reflections

Timelines are a useful way of looking at your life story:
Try to draw a line representing your life chronologically.
Have a go at identifying events or experiences that have been significant, both good and not so good.

I realise that in this chapter we have not explored a great deal about followers – for we could hardly lead without them, and this chapter will not make you a good leader. I hope though that it has led you to some thought about leadership. I have tried to explore some ideas behind the importance of leadership and why there is so much interest in the idea. The chapter has offered the idea of authentic leadership as particularly relevant to early years settings and has suggested some ways in which we might develop our authenticity as leaders. I give the closing words to Bolman and Deal (1997: 404):

> The need for leadership derives ultimately from the uncertainties and dangers built into the human condition …. Leaders are one source of help. They help us feel less fearful and more confident. They help us find attractive and plausible versions of what to think, feel and do.
>
> They help us to see possibilities and discover resources. Therein lies both the power and the risk of leadership. Leadership, like love, carries risk of both dependence and disappointment. We may look to leaders when we might better look to ourselves. We may follow false prophets. But it makes no more sense to reject leadership altogether than to shun all forms of intimacy. We need to approach both with a combination of hope and wisdom.

Reflections

Think about how well you meet these criteria (from Walumbwa et al., 2008) as an authentic leader:

Self-awareness:
Do you seek feedback to improve your interactions with others?
Can you accurately describe how others view your capabilities?
Relational transparency:
Do you say exactly what you mean?
Are you willing to admit mistakes when they are made?
Internalised moral perspective:
Do you demonstrate beliefs that are consistent with your actions?
Do you make decisions based on your core values?
Balanced processing:
Do you ask for views that challenge your deeply help positions?
Do you listen carefully to different points of view before coming to conclusions?

References

Antonakis J., Canciolo A. and Sternberg R. (2004). *The Nature of Leadership*. Thousand Oaks: Sage.
Aubrey, C. (2007). *Leading and Managing in the Early Years*. London: Sage.

Avolio, B. J., Gardner, W. L. and Walumbwa, F. O. (2005). Preface. In B. J. Avolio, W. L. Gardner and F. O. Walumbwa (Eds.), *Authentic Leadership Theory and Practice: Origins, Effects and Development*. Bingley: Emerald.

Bass, B. (1990). *Bass and Stogdill's Handbook of Leadership*. New York: Free Press.

Bolman, L. and Deal, T. (1997). *Reframing Organizations: Artistry, Choice and Leadership*. San Francisco: Jossey Bass [2nd Ed].

Booker, R. (2012). Leadership in children's services. *Children & Society*, 26 pp. 394–405.

Briggs, M. and Briggs, I. (2009). *Developing Your Leadership in the Early Years*. London: Bloomsbury.

Burns, J. (1978). *Leadership*. New York: Harper & Row.

Carlyle, A. (Ed.) (1904). New Letters of Thomas Carlyle, edited by A. Carlyle. 11, pp. 332–3.

Case, P., French, R. and Simpson, P. (2011) Philosophy of leadership. In: Bryman, A., Collinson, D., Jackson, B. and Uhl-Bien. M., eds. (2011) *Sage Handbook of Leadership*. London: Sage, pp. 685–727.

Dalli, C. (2005). *Reflecting on Professionalism in Early Years Teaching: Relationships, Responsiveness and Curriculum*. Early Years Lecture Series. Glasgow: University of Strathclyde.

Dalton, P. and Dunnett, G. (1992). *A Psychology for Living: Personal Construct Theory for Professionals and Clients*. Chichester: Wiley.

DeRue, D. Nahrgang, J., Wellman, N. and Humphrey, S. (2011) Trait and behavioral theories of leadership: An integration and meta-analytic test of their relative validity. *Personnel Psychology* 4 no. 1 pp. 7–52.

Dunlop, A. (2008). *A Literature Review on Leadership in the Early Years*. Glasgow: University of Strathclyde.

French, J. and Raven, B. (1959) The bases of social power. In D. Cartwright and A. Zander (eds.) *Group Dynamics*. New York: Harper and Row.

Friedman, M. (1970) The social responsibility of business is to increase its profits. *New York Times Magazine*, September 13.

Gardiner, R. (2011). A critique of the discourse of authentic leadership. *International Journal of Business and Social Science* 2 no. 15 pp 99–104.

Gardner, W. Cogliser, C. Davis, K. and Dickens, M. (2011). Authentic leadership: A review of the literature and research agenda. *The Leadership Quarterly* 22 pp. 1120–1145.

George, W. and Sims, P. (2007). *True North: Discover your Authentic Leadership*. San Francisco: Jossey-Bass.

Greenleaf, R. K. (1970). *The Servant as Leader*. Westfield, IN: Robert K. Greenleaf Publishing Centre.

Grint, K. (2010). *Leadership: Limits and Possibilities*. Basingstoke: Palgrave Macmillan.

Jackson, B. and Parry, K. (2008). *A Very Short, Fairly Interesting and Reasonably Cheap Book about Studying Leadership*. London: Sage.

Jones, C. and Pound, L. (2008) *Leadership and Management in the Early Years*. Maidenhead: McGraw-Hill International.

Kagan, S. and Hallmark, L. (2001). Cultivating leadership in early care and education. *Child Care Information Exchange* 140 pp. 7–10.

Leeson, C., Campbell-Barr, V. and Ho, D. (2012). Leading for quality improvement: a comparative research agenda in early childhood education in England and Hong Kong. *International Journal of Leadership in Education: Theory and Practice* 15 no. 2 pp 221–236.

Luft, J. and Ingham, H. (1955). *The Johari Window: A Graphic Model of Interpersonal Awareness*. Proceedings of the Western Training Laboratory in Group Development. Los Angeles: UCLA.

Luthans, F. and Avolio, B. (2003). Authentic leadership development. In K. S. Cameron, J. E. Dutton and R. E. Quinn (Eds.), *Positive Organizational Scholarship*, 241–258. San Francisco: Berrett-Koehler.

McDowall Clark, R. and Murray, J. (2012). *Reconceptualizing Leadership in the Early Years*. Maidenhead: Open University Press.

Middlehurst, R. (1993). *Leading Academics*. Maidenhead: SRHE and Open University Press.

Moyles, J. (2004). *Effective Leadership and Management in the Early Years*. Maidenhead: Open University Press/McGraw-Hill Education.

Northouse, P. (2016). *Leadership Theory and Practice*, 7th edn. Thousand Oaks, CA: Sage.

Osgood, J. (2006). Deconstructing professionalism in early childhood education: resisiting the regulatory gaze. *Contemporary Issues in Early Childhood*, 7 no. 1.

Rodd, J. (2013). *Leadership in Early Childhood*. 4th edn. Maidenhead: Open University Press.

Robins, A. and Callan, S. (2008). *Managing Early Years Settings: Supporting and Leading Teams*. London: Sage Publications.

Scrivens, C. (2002). Constructions of leadership: Does gender make a difference? Perspectives from an English speaking country In V. Nivala and E. Hujala (Eds.), *Leadership in Early Childhood Education, Cross Cultural Perspectives*. Oulu, Finland: University of Oulu.

Senge, P. (1994) *The Fifth Discipline Fieldbook*. New York: Doubleday.

Sharp, C., Lord, P., Handscomb, G., Macleod, S., Southcott, C., George, N. and Jeffes, J. (2012). *Highly Effective Leadership in Children's Centres*. Nottingham: National College for teaching and Leadership.

Solly, K. (2003). What do early years leaders do to maintain and enhance the significance of the early years? A paper on a conversation with Kathryn Solly held at the Institute of Education on 22 May 2003.

Walumbwa, F., Avolio, B., Gardner, W., Wernsing, T. and Peterson, S. (2008). Authentic leadership: development and validation of a theory-based measure. *Journal of Management* 34 pp 89–126.

Whitehead, G. (2009) Adolescent leadership development: building a case for an authenticity framework. *Educational Management Administration and Leadership* 37 no. 6 pp 847–872.

Part 2

Diversity and diverse philosophical ideas

The multicultural classroom
Celebrating diversity and challenging disparities

Ami Montgomery

Overview

This chapter considers perspectives on culture and how these impact on the multicultural classroom. The dimensions of a multicultural education are explored, including content integration, transformative curriculum, prejudice reduction, an equity pedagogy and an empowering school culture and social structure.

Introduction

As cultural diversity continues to grow, so should we. With the world becoming increasingly globalised and amid the intensification of cultural diversity in societies, educational settings face the crucial challenge of ensuring that schools develop a social climate where cultural diversity is "respected and seen as a resource rather than a burden or a threat" (Civitillo et al. 2017: 1). Over the past several decades, cultural diversity in the classroom has been an area of significant interest amongst scholars concerned with education. It continues to be of particular importance when researching gaps in educational attainment for learners from diverse home backgrounds and those with English as an Additional Language (EAL). Historically, researchers have sought to identify those underlying causes of underachievement by examining the 'deficiencies' found in a learner's home background and focusing on the aspects lacking from their home life. However, over time we see that researchers are now approaching this area of study with a more positive view of diversity. It can now be seen in educational research that diverse cultures truly enrich our society and contribute a unique 'salad bowl' effect to our classroom dynamics (Kalen 1924, Bourne 1916, and Drachsler 1920, cited in Banks 2016: 44). As educational policy outlines, it is imperative for all learners to succeed academically, irrespective of their background. To assure this, it is essential for all educators to draw on the positive aspects of cultural diversity, valuing learners' cultural and linguistic resources as capital to build upon, as opposed to seeing them as a barrier to learning. With this in mind, educators are consequently faced with a need for change and a call for a position of cultural pluralism to be evidenced at all levels of education (Bonner et al. 2017), not only in the teaching practices of our classrooms but in both educational and public policies. Furthermore, it is equally important to consider some of the more difficult issues that many marginalised learners, and their teachers, face on a daily basis.

Reflections

How have you promoted a notion of diversity with the young children you are involved with?

Have you met any difficulties?

Have did you overcome them to promote understanding of a diverse community?

In this chapter I explore the current challenges faced by teachers in the multicultural classroom and the significance of celebrating cultural diversity whilst challenging those disparities found amongst our learners through practice, adopting a more culturally responsive pedagogy.

The significance of culture

The term "culture" can be problematic, due to the abundance of definitions proposed over the years (Baldwin et al. 2006), frequently meaning different things to different people. It is inevitable that pre-determined ideas and beliefs contribute to someone's culture. Kroeber and Kluckhohn's 1952 comprehensive study identifies over 160 definitions of culture, with the following most popular amongst the social sciences:

> ...culture consists of patterns, explicit and implicit, of and for behaviour acquired and transmitted by symbols, constituting the distinctive achievements of human groups, including their embodiments in artefacts; the essential core of culture consists of traditional (i.e. historically derived and selected) ideas and especially attached values.
>
> (Kroeber and Kluckhohn 1952: 161)

Operating a traditional definition as the "higher forms of knowledge" (Scheler 1960: 31–60), early views of culture allowed for a distinction between "civilised" and "primitive" or "tribal" cultures, each ethnic group possessing a distinct worldview that is incommensurable with the worldview of other groups. Later philosophical definitions of culture adopted a more inclusive view of culture, where all societies were believed to share a set of "elementary ideas", an ideal of individual human refinement and a pursuit of total perfection (Arnold, 1960 [1869]), but where different cultures cultivate local modifications of these elementary ideas (Bastian (1826–1905), cited in Kopping, 2005).

Culture has most recently been defined within the field of sociological research as something linked to more meaningful and symbolic actions, emphasising the most important aspects of culture as the intangible, symbolic and ideational aspects of group life. Culture is often explored through the dynamic and systematic processes in which meanings are created and reflected in human interaction with symbols (Samovar et al. 2010), in a particular time and place. "Culture is not itself visible, but is made visible only through its representation" (Maanen 2011: 3), expressed by the behaviour and language of participants which in turn is construed by the fieldworker – an interpretive act by a scholar that occurs with the writing of texts, through self-consciously written words. It is often problematic for researchers to truly know of the cultures present due to their simple reliance on inference and speculation about what they observe (Wagner 1981).

The complexity of culture further intensifies when we consider the context or setting that the learners occupy. This in turn contributes to further cultural choices made by the learner. The cultural groups to which they belong, for example, can influence the basis for categorisation and the formation of in-groups and out-groups, especially in an institutional context in which these groups have differential status and power (Lotan 2012). Cultural similarity provides attributional confidence, a means of operationalising uncertainty through the process of defining the measurement of a phenomenon that is not directly measurable, in this case culture, which consequently reduces uncertainty. Highly dissimilar cultures often exhibit differences in communication patterns, value dimensions and friendship styles that can impede relationship development, and in turn educational attainment.

Culture is complex and interchangeable, dependent on endlessly shifting variables. Although no one theory can provide all the answers to educational concerns that arise with learning and teaching in multicultural settings, sociocultural theories provide stimulating insights into these problems for our consideration. Traditionally, educators would consider culture as distinct from learning, except in the most superficial of ways. By this I mean that learning would appear "divorced from the influence of native culture" (Nieto 2010 1). However, it is now evident that a deeper understanding of race, culture and ethnicity is essential in education for effective learning.

The multicultural classroom

Whether you teach in a large urban public school system, a small rural schoolhouse, or an affluent private academy in the suburbs, you will face learners who are more diverse than ever in terms of race, language background, ethnicity, culture and other differences.

(Nieto 2010: xi)

A range of cultures in educational settings is a true asset; learners bring with them different languages, backgrounds and faiths. Differing cultural perspectives provide a dynamic and vivid opportunity for debate and the need for mutual respect adds to the general dignity of the environment. However, multicultural education does not simply involve the affirmation of language and culture, but should additionally view these matters critically and challenge "issues of power and privilege in society" (Nieto 2010: 39).

As we know, education is influenced by the social, political, historical and economic context in which it takes place, "structures that frame and define our society" (Nieto 2010: 38). Despite this, education is often approached in isolation from the socio-political contexts presented above, ignoring the ideologies and myths that shape commonly accepted ideas and values in society. This results in a singular focus on cultural artefacts, disconnected from the actual lives of those involved (Nieto 2010). Schools are seen as "arenas of intercultural tension" (Forrest et al. 2017: 17) where children spend a significant amount of time interacting with their peers in cross-cultural circumstances (Guerra, Williams and Sadek 2011) and schools are essential to the development of communication strategies aimed at multicultural understanding (MacLaren and Torres 1999). It is the time spent interacting with their peers in cross-cultural circumstances that is essential for multicultural understanding.

It is additionally within this linguistic landscape where children learn about their own cultural identity, framing "how one experiences the world" (Nieto 2010: 39), and develop a sense of belonging in a multicultural society surrounded by diverse cultures. Multicultural classrooms must thrive on the differences and uniqueness of their learners and use them as an underpinning for development and growth.

It is becoming increasingly recognised that culture and cultural differences play a discernible role in learning. Learning can take place in a fairly uncomplicated manner when a learner's home cultural values and behaviours mirror those of the educational setting. A learner's home can be seen as the first context for learning, where they not only learn to walk and talk but learn how to learn. However when these cultural values do not "fit" with school policies and practices (Nieto 2010: 148) this can be problematic. Ramirez and Castañeda (1974), in their early research on child-rearing practices, found that the child-rearing styles of caregivers from diverse cultures resulted in different learning styles among their children, diverse approaches to receiving and processing information. As a result, they suggest that learning environments should be created to reflect these diverse learning styles and should be more culturally democratic. Learners need to feel safe, settled, valued and secure; they need a sense of belonging, where learning builds on what they know, understand and what they can do. Schools should recognise the positive contribution that diverse cultures can make to the school and it is important for these cultures to be positively reflected in the school. For those learners with English as an additional language (EAL), there is an initial expectation that they should cast off their home language, "wounding the spirit" (Locust 1988: 315), and therefore it is even more important for their home culture to be celebrated and embraced. A key aspect of multicultural education is the importance of addressing cultural disparities in an attempt to overcome unfair inequalities in educational attainment.

To be effective in this, multicultural education needs to take account of the "history of immigration, the social, political and economic inequality and exclusion" characterising education, past and present (Nieto 2010: 39), and move beyond diversity. Multicultural education aims to assist learners in developing the "knowledge, attitudes and skills needed to function within their own [and] other micro-cultures, and within the global community" (Banks 2001: 25) and supports the specific needs of learners for whom their language background is something other than English (Bianco 2010; Inglis 2009).

Reflections

How can knowledge of different cultures be incorporated into activities with young children?
Which strategies have you found most effective?

Rooted in their high power status within schools, teachers have a crucial role in addressing cultural sensitivities and multicultural values and ensuring that all learners are socially integrated. Once more, teachers are required to modify attitudes regarding differences and inequalities amongst cultures within their classrooms and those differences among cultures present in their own practice. This is particularly important in rural and regional areas of the UK which are largely 'white' linguistic landscapes: "to agree to learn from a stranger who does not respect your integrity causes a major loss of self" (Kohl 1994: 6). Most teachers are sincerely concerned with providing all learners in their class with the best education possible and with ensuring their academic success. However, due to limits to their own educational experiences, they may know little about the differences amongst those they teach, often referring back to spurious assumptions and stereotypes about their students' diverse backgrounds. Furthermore teachers are often removed from the development of educational policies and practices in the schools in which they work, and consequently become the products of educational systems which can be both harmful and oppressive to many of their culturally diverse learners.

Culturally Responsive Teaching (CRT) is a pedagogy incorporated by teachers who recognise the true importance of embracing learners' cultural references in all aspects of their learning. This includes acknowledging, responding to and celebrating all cultures (Ladson-Billings 1994). It has evolved from a growing body of research originating in the 1970s which was further developed in the 1990s.

It offers diverse learners full and equitable access to education and ensures they achieve through the support of their teachers. This pedagogy embraces respect for all cultural backgrounds, appropriate communication and effective instructional strategies,

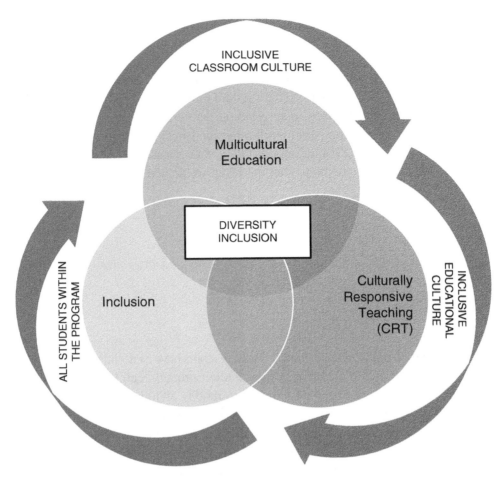

Figure 4.1 Culturally responsive teaching pedagogy
The Diversity Inclusive Program Model (LaVergne, 2008)

developing meaningful connections to the curriculum (Irvine and Armento 2001). Teachers who embrace a culturally responsive approach to teaching apply interactive, collaborative teaching methods, strategies and ways of interacting that support cultural and linguistic differences for learners from diverse backgrounds; see Figure 4.1.

Many research projects have been developed in the hope of advancing educational systems and practices so as to "increase learner academic achievement and improve intergroup skills" (Banks 2016: 297). This is often seen as benefiting only learners who are from an ethnic minority; however, it becomes clear with practice that this has benefits for all.

Educational settings are the "microcosm of society" (Priest 2014 cited in Forrest et al. 2017: 17) where learners negotiate those intercultural tensions which they have experienced within the wider environment, one of those tensions being academic attainment. The gap in attainment between majority and minority learners is once more indicative of the struggles to advance educational equity (Banks 2009). The academic achievement gap is used to describe the circumstances in which learners from diverse backgrounds, primarily racially, culturally and linguistically marginalised backgrounds, achieve significantly less than other learners. Two major causes of the academic achievement gap have been associated with sociocultural and school-related factors (D'Amico 2001). Whilst sociocultural factors include poverty, ethnicity, parents' low level of education, family support systems etc., school-related factors include low expectations. This educational context is unfair to many young learners. The problem with the term "academic achievement gap" is that it suggests that rather than resting with unequal schooling, the problem is in fact a "minority" issue, where the learners alone are responsible for their learning and the gap in their educational attainment. Multicultural education aims to address these school-related issues to improve the context of schools for these learners. Educators can do little to change the life circumstances of learners, but "well-trained and motivated teachers" (Nieto 2010: 48) can narrow the achievement gap by delivering a culturally sensitive and challenging curriculum.

Effective dimensions of multicultural education

We need to continually remind ourselves that multiculturalism is not just about expanding individual horizons, or increasing personal intercultural skills, but is part of a larger project...

(Kymlicka 1995 cited in Nieto 2010: 45)

Diversity and differences command work, resolution, openness and understanding. For those teachers who address and embed this into their practice, a learning environment will be successfully created to advance the educational goals of all learners. However, there is limited agreement on how educational settings should shape their learning environments to address cultural diversity (Thijs and Verkuyten 2014) or about the practices and artefacts teachers should adopt to develop a "warm and supportive environment for learners' individual needs" (Gay 2010 cited in Civitillo et al, 2017: 2). It has been proposed that it is essential for teachers to successfully identify, differentiate and understand what it means to teach in a classroom that is multicultural. Teacher's knowledge, skills and dispositions concerning effective support for those in their classrooms, along with their beliefs about and abilities to educate diverse learners, are essential to those learners' academic success, and linked to positive academic attainment for immigrant and ethnic minority learners (Aronson and Laughter 2016). Over the past few decades there have been significant writings about teachers' inadequate preparation, in terms of cultivating relevant content knowledge, experience and training (Au 2009; Cummins 2007), and about their reluctance to broach issues of difference, both among themselves and their learners (Fine, 1992; Jervis, 1996; McIntyre, 1997; Sleeter, 1994; Solomon, 1995; Tatum, 1997). Often resulting in a cultural gap between teachers and their learners (Gay 2010), inadequate preparation can limit the teacher's ability to employ effective practices to accommodate the cultural and linguistic characteristics of diverse learners (Orosco 2010, Orosco and O'Connor 2011). Nieto (2010) reminds us that we may not always have the answers to educational issues, and that some of the answers that we do have are in fact incorrect: "we are all embedded in our own procedures, which makes us both very smart in one situation and blind and stupid in the next" (McDermott 1977: 202).

Before discussing the effective dimensions of multicultural education further it is imperative that we acknowledge that differing goals for multicultural education may be emphasised in practice. The goal emphasised is dependent on one's conceptualisation of multicultural education. Any consensus about the nature, aims and scope of the field of multicultural education, among specialists and in the heated discourse among non-specialists (Gray 1991; Leo 1990; Schlesinger 1991), is generally obscured. Nieto highlights that education must confront inequality and stratification in schools and society and asserts that:

> no educational philosophy or program is worthwhile unless it focuses on three primary concerns:
>
> 1. Tackling inequality and promoting access to an equal education
> 2. Raising the achievement of all learners and providing them with an equitable and high-quality education
> 3. Giving learners an apprenticeship in the opportunity to become critical and productive members of a democratic society.
>
> (Nieto 2010: 44)

If multicultural education is to be better understood and implemented by practitioners in ways more consistent with theory, its various dimensions must be more clearly described, conceptualised and researched (Banks 2004). Multicultural education is presented in Figure 4.2 below as a field consisting of five dimensions, as formulated in the work of James Banks (2012b).

Although each dimension is conceptually distinct, in practice they overlap and are interrelated. All educators should be able to identify, differentiate and understand the meanings of each of the five dimensions, discussed in more detail in the following section, for successful implementation.

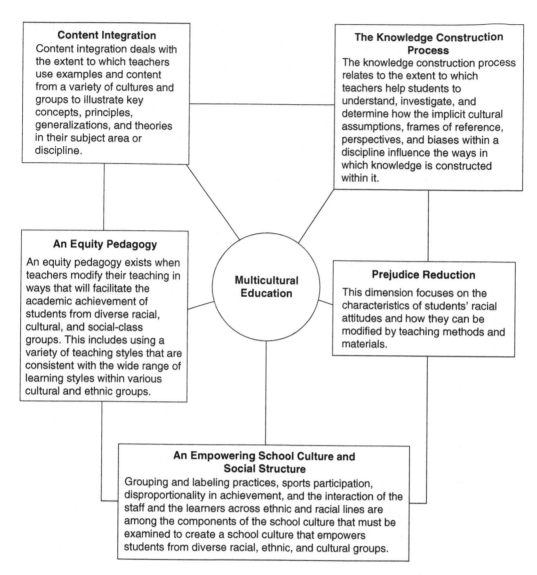

Figure 4.2 Dimensions of Multicultural Education (Banks 2016: 6)

Content integration

The first of the five dimensions is content integration. Content integration deals with the extent to which educators incorporate content and specific examples from diverse cultures and groups to illustrate learning objectives, concepts and principles. This can be seen in Banks' work discussing curriculum reform and how U.S. educators embedded curriculum content which included African Americans, Mexican Americans and Asian Americans.

The common belief that content integration constitutes the foundations of multicultural education has been a key factor that has caused many subject teachers of mathematics and science to view multicultural education negatively. Many such teachers see it as an endeavour primarily for social studies and language arts teachers, in whose work there are frequent and ample opportunities to use ethnic and cultural content to illustrate concepts, themes and principles. For example Banks (2012) discusses the opportunities provided by the language arts, where learners can examine the ways in which Ebonics (Black English) is both similar to and different from mainstream U.S. English (Alim and Smitherman 2012; Hudley and Mallinson 2011).

Irrespective of subject, for effective content integration, the infusion of cultural content into the curriculum area should be logical and not tenuous and contrived.

The knowledge construction process

The knowledge construction process consists of the methods, activities and questions teachers use to help their learners understand, investigate, and determine how implicit cultural assumptions, frames of reference, perspectives and biases influence the ways in which knowledge is constructed. When the knowledge construction process is implemented effectively, learners can understand how knowledge is created and influenced by *positionality*, the influence of the racial, ethnic and social-class positions of individuals and groups (Harding 2012).

Whist researchers within each academic discipline stress the importance of formulating knowledge without the influence of the personal or cultural characteristics (Myrdal 1969), critical theorists highlight how personal, cultural and social factors influence the formulation of knowledge even when objective knowledge is the ideal within a discipline (Banks 1996; Collins 2000). Personal experiences and positions within society influence the knowledge we produce.

It is important for teachers, in addition to their learners, to understand how knowledge is constructed across disciplines. The disciplines are often taught "as a body of truth not to be questioned or critically analysed" (Banks, 1996). However, multicultural education stresses that learners need to understand how cultural assumptions, perspectives and frames of reference influence the questions that researchers ask and the conclusions, generalisations and principles they formulate.

Transformative curriculum: the multicultural way

When considering the knowledge construction dimension of multicultural education in our classrooms it is equally important to consider transforming the curriculum as part of a whole school approach. The transformative curriculum changes the basic assumptions of the curriculum and enables learners to view concepts, issues, themes and problems from diverse ethnic and cultural perspectives (Banks 1993). This new approach to the curriculum encourages learners to consider the author's purposes for writing or speaking, his or her basic assumptions, and how the author's perspective or point of view compares with that of other authors and resources. It is within this process that learners will develop lifelong skills, equipping them for everyday life and not just to meet the demands of academic tests.

Prejudice reduction

The prejudice reduction dimension of multicultural education describes the characteristics of learners' racial attitudes and the strategies that can be used to help them develop increasingly more representative attitudes and values. The characteristics of children's racial attitudes towards diversity and culture has been an area of significant interest for researchers since the 1920s (Lasker 1929). Historically, research highlights how young children would enter school with negative racial attitudes that mirror those of adults (Aboud 1988; Stephan and Stephan 2001) and stresses how effective curricular interventions can help learners develop more positive racial and gender attitudes (Levy and Killen 2008; Stephan and Stephan 2001). This dimension may seem odd in the twenty-first century, especially as we consider the multicultural settings and scenarios we find ourselves in on a daily basis. However, in some educational settings this is still an area for further development.

Since the 1940s, a number of studies have explored curriculum interventions in the U.S. to determine the effects of more inclusive teaching practices, multicultural materials, role playing and other kinds of simulated experiences on the racial attitudes and perceptions of learners. These studies indicate that under certain conditions curriculum interventions can assist learners to develop more positive racial and ethnic attitudes (Aboud 2009; Stephan and Vogt 2004) and provide guidelines for teachers to assist with the improvement of classroom practice. When teachers encourage extra- and co-curricular activities they can create rich possibilities for structuring superordinate groups and cross-cutting group memberships. Previous studies indicate the contributions of intergroup relations (Banks et al. 2001; Bigler and Hughes 2009; Stephan and Stephan 2004): "When membership in superordinate groups is salient, other group differences become less important" (Banks 2001: 9). Theory indicates that when learners from diverse cultural, racial, and language groups share a superordinate identity, such as being members of the football team, film club, choir, Girl Scouts etc., cultural boundaries weaken: "creating superordinate groups stimulates cohesion, which can mitigate pre-existing animosities" (Banks 2001; 9). Learners are consequently able to form friendships and to have positive interactions and relationships with learners from different racial, cultural, language, and religious groups. For these groups to be effective it is essential that the integrity of different cultures is represented in the classroom and is respected and given legitimacy, as groups that reflect only the norms and values of the dominant and powerful groups within the school are not likely to improve intergroup relations.

Over the last three decades much time has been spent studying the effects of this approach to cooperative learning on the academic achievement of learners from different racial and ethnic groups (Aronson and Gonzalez 1988; Cohen 1972; Cohen and Lotan 2004; Slavin 1979). Research surrounding the effect of this dimension has been significantly influenced by the work of Allport (1954), who hypothesised that prejudice would be reduced if multicultural contact situations had the following characteristics:

1. They are cooperative rather than competitive;
2. The individuals experience equal status;
3. The individuals have shared goals; and
4. The contact is sanctioned by authorities such as parents, the principal and the teacher.

Reflections

How do you ensure racism is not part of your setting?

What are the most effective strategies to promote an atmosphere where all are valued?

What special requirements do you consider for individuals of a different religious background?

An equity pedagogy

An equity pedagogy exists when practitioners modify their teaching practice in ways that will facilitate the academic achievement of learners from diverse racial, cultural, ethnic, language and gender groups (Gay 2010; Howard 2010; Nieto 2010). As highlighted in the research, teachers can increase the classroom participation and academic achievement of learners from different cultural groups by modifying their instruction so that it draws on their cultural and language strengths.

Darling-Hammond (2010) indicates that the academic achievement of learners from diverse ethnic and low-income backgrounds increases when they have high-quality teachers who are experts in their curriculum subject, pedagogy and child development. She reports on a particular study conducted by Gamoran and Dreeben (1986), who found that when African American learners received high-quality instruction, their reading achievement was as high as that of white learners.

Further theories developed within the field of equity pedagogy indicate that teachers can improve the school success of learners when they are knowledgeable about the cultures, values, language and learning characteristics of the learners in their class.

An empowering school culture and social structure

This dimension of multicultural education involves restructuring the culture and organisation of the school so that learners from diverse racial, ethnic and gender groups will experience equality. This variable must be examined and addressed as part of a whole school approach, including the head teacher and all support staff at the educational setting. In order to determine the subtle messages given to learners about racial, ethnic, cultural and social-class diversity, the behaviour of the school staff and an examination of the covert and visible culture and organisation of the school needs to be fully explored to determine the extent to which it nurtures or obstructs educational equity.

Like all classification schemas, the approach that considers the five dimensions of multicultural education has both strengths and limitations. The dimensions typology provides a useful framework for categorising and interpreting the extensive literature on cultural diversity, ethnicity and education. The typology of the dimensions is an ideal-type conception as it approaches the complexity of the reality of the multiculturalism classroom without describing it in its total complexity. Despite their helpfulness as conceptual tools, providing a way to organise and make sense of complex and distinct data and observations, the five categories are "interrelated and overlapping, not mutually exclusive" (Banks 2016: 6). Content integration, for example, describes any approach used to integrate content about racial and cultural groups into the curriculum. The knowledge construction process describes a method in which teachers help learners to understand how knowledge is created and how it reflects the experiences of various ethnic, racial, cultural and language groups. As with the majority of new pedagogical approaches, guidelines and framework tools, practitioners are required to consider the suggested dimensions outlined above in light of their own learners and educational settings.

Conclusion

Multicultural education is a way of viewing reality and a way of thinking about, and not just content about, various ethnic, racial and cultural groups. Publications continue to be circulated to provide teachers with the examples and specifics needed to effectively integrate and embrace cultural diversity into their teaching. Teachers can learn about and think of new ways in which they can modify their teaching and implement equity pedagogy in their classrooms (Banks 1991).

Multicultural education, as discussed in this chapter, aims to reform educational practice to ensure that learners from diverse home backgrounds experience educational equality, irrespective of culture, be that in schools, colleges or universities. The significant growth in multicultural educational research, policy and practice over the past three decades is captured in Banks' 2009 and 2012 publications, The *Routledge International Companion* to *Multicultural Education* and the *Encyclopaedia of Diversity in Education*. Furthermore, these publications present the variety of perspectives, typologies and conceptual schemas which have been developed in the field to explore the aims and scopes of multicultural education. Many concepts have emerged to describe the educational practices related to cultural differences reflecting different and conflicting "goals, approaches and strategies" (Banks 2016: 71). However, the dimensions of multicultural education hold true for most: we must embrace and celebrate the cultural diversity of all of our learners and ensure that any cultural disparities are challenged to secure their academic success.

Developing a multicultural approach in our classrooms will not eliminate the inequalities present, and is by no means the "panacea" (Nieto 2010: 61) for all multicultural matters; however, courage, creativity, hard work and ongoing collaboration to embrace multicultural education has the promise to help.

References

Aboud, F. (2009). Modifying children's racial attitudes. In J. A. Banks (Ed.), *The Routledge International Companion to Multicultural Education*. New York: Routledge.

Aboud, F. E. (1988). *Children and Prejudice*. New York: Blackwell Press.

Alim, H. S. and Smitherman, G. (2012). *Articulate While Black: Barack Obama, Language, and Race in the U.S.* New York, NY: Oxford University Press.

Allport, G. W. (1954). *The Nature of Prejudice*. Garden City, NY: Doubleday.

Aronson, B. and Laughter, J. (2016). The theory and practice of culturally relevant Education: A synthesis of research across content areas. *Review of Educational Research*, 86, 237–276. http://dx.doi.org/10.3102/0034654315582066.

Aronson, E. and Gonzalez, A. (1988). Desegregation, jigsaw, and the Mexican-American experience. In P. A. Katz and D. A. Taylor, (Eds.), *Eliminating Racism: Profiles in Controversy*. New York: Plenum Press.

Arnold, M. (1960 [1869]) Culture and anarchy: an essay in political and social criticism. In J. H. Super (Ed.), *The Complete Prose Works of Matthew Arnold*. 9 volumes, 1960–73.Vol. 5. Ann Arbor: University of Michigan Press.

Au, K. (2009). Isn't culturally responsive instruction just good teaching? *Social Education*, 73(4), 279–283.

Baldwin, J. R., Faulkner, S. L., Hecht, M. L. and Lindsley, S. L. (2006). Definitions of culture. Cited in J. R. Baldwin, S. L. Faulkner, M. L. Hecht and S. L. Lindsley (Eds.), *Redefining Culture: Perspectives Across the Disciplines* (pp. 139–226). Mahwah, NJ: Taylor & Francis.

Banks, J. A. (2016). *Cultural Diversity and Education. Foundations, Curriculum and Teaching*. New York: NY; Routledge.

Banks, J. A. (2012). *Encyclopaedia of Diversity in Education* (4 vols.). Thousand Oaks, CA: Sage Publications.

Banks, J. A. (2009). *The Routledge International Companion to Multicultural Education*. London and New York: Routledge.

Banks, J. A. (2004). Multicultural education: historical developments, dimensions, and practice. In J. A. Banks and C. A. M. Banks (Eds.), *Handbook of Research in Multicultural Education* (pp. 3–30). San Francisco: Jossey Bass.

Banks, J. (2001). Multicultural education: characteristics and goals. In J. Banks and C. A. McGee (Eds.), *Multicultural Education: Issues and Perspectives*, 4th Ed., New York: Wiley, pp. 3–26. https://doi.org/10.1016/b0-08-043076-7/02390-1

Banks, J. A., Cookson, P., Gay, G., Hawley, W.D., Irvine, J. J., Nieto, S., Schofield, J. W. and Stephan, W. G. (2001). *Diversity within unity: Essential principles for teaching and learning in a multicultural society*. Seattle: Center for Multicultural Education, University of Washington.

Banks, J. A. (Ed.) (1996). Multicultural Education, Transformative Knowledge and Action. New York: Teachers College Press.

Banks, J. A. (1993). Multicultural education: historical development, dimensions, and practice. In *Review of Research in Education* 19.

Banks, J. A. (1991). The dimensions of multicultural education. *Multicultural Leader*, 4, 5–6.

Bianco, J.L. (2010). The importance of language policies and multilingualism for cultural diversity. *International Social Science Journal* 61, no. 19, 37–67.

Bigler, R. and Hughes, J. (2009). The nature and origins of children's racial attitudes. In J. Banks (Ed.) *The Routledge International Companion to Multicultural Education*. New York: Routledge, pp. 186–198.

Bonner, P. J., Warren, S. R. and Jiang, Y. H. (2017). Voices from urban classrooms: teachers' perceptions on instructing diverse learners and using culturally responsive teaching. *Education and Urban Society*. 1–30. DOI: 10. 1177/0013124517713820

Bourne, R. (1916) Trans-national America. *The Atlantic* 118.

Civitillo, S., Schachner, M., Juang, L., Vijver, F, J, R., Handrick, A. and Noack, P. (2017). Towards a better understanding of cultural diversity approaches at school: A multi-informant and mixed-methods study. *Learning, Culture and Social Interaction* 12, 1–14.

Cohen, E.G., and Lotan, R.A. (2004). Equity in heterogeneous classrooms. In J.A. Banks and C.A.M. Banks (Eds.), *Handbook of Research on Multicultural Education*, 2nd ed. San Francisco, CA: Jossey-Bass, pp. 736–752.

Cohen, E. G. (1972). Interracial interaction disability. *Human Relations*, 25(1), 9–24.

Collins, P. H. (2000). *Black Feminist Thought: Knowledge, Consciousness, and the Politics of Empowerment*. New York: Routledge.

Cummins, J. (2007). Pedagogies for the poor? Realigning reading instruction for low-income learners with scientifically based reading research. *Educational Research*, 36(9), 564–572. Doi: 10.3102/0013189X07313156.

D'Amico, J. (2001). A closer look at the minority achievement gap. *ERS Spectrum*, 19(2), 4–10.

Darling-Hammond, L. (2010). *The Flat World and Education: How America's Commitment to Equity Will Determine our Future*. New York, NY: Teachers College Press.

Drachsler, J. (1920). *Democracy and Assimilation: The Blending of Immmigrant Heritages in America*. New York: The MacMillan Company.

Fine, M. (1992). *Disruptive Voices*. Ann Arbor: University of Michigan Press.

Forrest, J., Lean, G., and Dunn, K. (2017). Attitudes of classroom teachers to cultural diversity and multicultural education in country New South Wales, Australia. *Australian Journal of Teacher Education*, 42(5).

Gamoran, A. and Dreeben, R. (1986) Coupling and control in educational organisations. *Administrative Science Quarterly* 31(4), 612–632.

Kalen, H. M. (1924) *Culture and Democracy in the United States*. New York: Boni and Liveright.

Kohl, H. (1994). *"I Won't Learn From You" and Other Thoughts on Creative Maladjustment*. New York: The New Press.

Gay, G. (2010). *Culturally Responsive Teaching: Theory, Research and Practice.* 2nd edn. New York: Teachers College Press.

Gray, P. (1991). *Whose America?* Cited in Banks, J. (1993). The canon debate. *Knowledge Construction and Multicultural Education* 22(5), 4–14.

Guerra, N. G., Williams, K. R., and Sadek, S. (2011). Understanding bullying and victimisation during childhood and adolescence: a mixed methods study. *Child Development*, 82, 295–310. https://doi.org/10.1111/j.1467-8624.2010.01556.x

Harding, S. (2012). Objectivity and diversity. In J. A. Banks (Ed.), *Encyclopedia of Diversity in Education* vol. 3. Thousand Oaks, CA: Sage Publications, pp. 1625–1630.

Howard, J. (2010). *Lazarus Rising: A Personal and Political Biography.* Sydney, NSW: HarperCollins

Hudley, A. C. and Mallinson, C. (2011). *Understanding English Language Variation in U.S. Schools.* New York: Teachers College Press.

Inglis, C. (2009). Multicultural education in Australia: two generations of evolution. In J. A. Banks (Ed.), *The Routledge International Companion to Multicultural Education.* New York: Routledge, pp. 109–120.

Irvine, J. J., and Armento, B. J. (2001). *Culturally Responsive Teaching: Lesson Planning for Elementary and Middle Grades.* New York, NY: McGraw-Hill.

Jervis, K. (1996). "How come there are no brothers on that list?": Hearing the hard questions all children ask. *Harvard Educational Review* 66, 546–576.

Kopping, K.-P. (2005) *Adolf Bastian and the Psychic Unity of Mankind: The Foundations of Anthropology in Nineteenth Century Germany.* Munster: Li Verlag. Re-edition of original edition by University of Queensland Press, 1983.

Kroeber, A. L. and Kluckhohn, C. (1952). *Culture: A Critical Review of Concepts and Definitions.* New York, NY: Vintage.

Kymlicka, W. (1995). *Multicultural Citizenship: A Liberal Theory of Minority rights.* New York, NY: Oxford University Press.

Ladson-Billings, G. (1994). *The Dream Keepers.* San Francisco: Jossey-Bass Publishing Co.

Lasker, B. (1929). *Race Attitudes in Children.* New York: Holt, Rinehart & Winston.

LaVergne, D. D. (2008). *Perceptions of Texas agricultural education teachers regarding diversity inclusion in secondary agricultural education programs* (Unpublished doctoral dissertation). Texas A&M University, College Station, TX.

Leo, J. (1990). A fringe history of the world. U. S. News and World Report, 12 November.

Levy, S. and Killen, M. (2008). *Intergroup Attitudes and Relations in Childhood through Adulthood.* Oxford: Oxford University Press.

Locust, C. (1988). Wounding the spirit: Discrimination and traditional American Indian belief systems. *Harvard Educational Review*, 3, 315–330.

Lotan, R. (2012). Complex instruction. In J. A. Banks (Ed.). *Cultural Diversity and Education. Foundations, Curriculum and Teaching.* New York: Routledge.

Maanen, J. V. (2011). *Tales of the Field: One Writing Ethnography.* 2nd ed. Chicago and London: University of Chicago Press.

MacLaren, P. and Torres, R. (1999). Racism and multicultural education: rethinking 'race' and 'whiteness' in late capitalism. In S. May (Ed.) *Critical Multiculturalism: Rethinking Multicultural and Antiracist Education* (pp. 46–83). London: Falmer Press.

McDermott, R. P. (1977). Social relations as contexts for learning in schools. *Harvard Educational Review.* 47(2), 198–213.

McIntyre, A. (1997). *Making Meaning of Whiteness.* Albany: State University of New York Press.

Myrdal, G. (1969) Investment in man. *International Social Work Journal*, 12(4), 2–15.

Nieto, S. (2010). *Language, Culture, and Teaching: Critical Perspectives*. Routledge

Orosco, M. J. (2010). Sociocultural considerations when using RtI with English language learners. *Theory into Practice*, 49(4), 265–272.

Orosco, M. J. and O'Connor, R. E. (2011). Cultural responsive instruction for English language learners with learning disabilities. *Journal of Learning Disabilities*. Advance online publication. Doi: 10.1177/0022219413476553.

Priest, N. (2014). Racism rife in schools, finds study. *Sydney Morning Herald*. 13 April.

Ramirez, M. and Castañeda, A. (1974). *Cultural Democracy, Bi-cognitive Development, and Education*. New York: Academic Press.

Samovar, L. A., Porter, R. E. and McDaniel, E. R. (2010). *Communication Between Cultures*. 7th ed. Belmont, CA: Wadsworth/Cengage Learning.

Scheler, M. (1960) *On the Eternal Man*. Translated by B. Noble. London: SCM Press.

Schlesinger, A. (1991). When ethnic studies are un-American. *Wall Street Journal*. 23 April.

Slavin, R. E. (1979). Effects of biracial learning teams on cross-racial friendships. *Journal of Educational Psychology*, 71(3), 381–387. http://dx.doi.org/10.1037/0022-0663.71.3.381

Sleeter, C. (1994). White racism. *Multicultural Education* 1(4), 5–8.

Solomon, R. P. (1995). Beyond prescriptive pedagogy: Teacher inservice education for cultural diversity. *Journal of Teacher Education* 46(4): 251–258.

Stephan, W. G., and Vogt, W. P. (Eds.) (2004). *Education Programs for Improving Intergroup Relations: Theory, Research, and Practice*. New York: Teachers College Press.

Stephan, W. G. and Stephan, C. W. (2001). *Improving Intergroup Relations*. Thousand Oaks, CA: Sage.

Tatum, B. D. (1997) *'Why Are All the Black Kids Sitting Together in the Cafeteria?' And Other Conversations about Race*. New York: Basic Books

Thijs, J. and Verkuyten, M. (2014). School ethnic diversity and learners' interethnic relations. *British Journal of Educational Psychology*, 84, 1–21. http://dx.doi.org/10.1111/bjep.12032.

Wagner, R. (1981). *The Invention of Culture*. Chicago: University of Chicago Press.

5 Creating and thinking critically

Pat Beckley

Overview

The chapter discusses strategies to encourage children to consider ideas in depth and to promote philosophical challenges that encourage them to generate their own decisions, analysis, evaluations and views. Adult interactions and the importance of questioning and listening to children's voices will be highlighted, along with reference to Bloom's taxonomy (see Figure 5.1).

How does creating and thinking critically concern philosophy as put into practice? This chapter is focused on children's philosophy, rather than how the adult thinks philosophically in ways that inform their approaches and beliefs about their involvement with young children. The Institute for the Advancement of Philosophy for Children (IAPC), considering the question 'What is philosophy for children?,' responds 'This is in itself an important philosophical question, not easy to answer: but let us say that philosophy, among other things, is a self-conscious inquiry into the meaning of puzzling and contestable concepts' (IAPC, n.d.) This 'self-conscious inquiry' encompasses creating and critical thinking. The IAPC continues, 'Philosophy is known for its cultivation of excellent thinking. One of the most ancient branches of philosophy is logic which includes… critical thinking.' Philosophy helps us to explore our experiences and for those of the children. The IAPC notes 'a major aim of education should be to help children become more reasonable—the 'Fourth R,' so perhaps philosophy should equally be part of the curriculum as reading, writing and arithmetic. This reflects a consideration of 'Values' as a way of sharing philosophical beliefs.'

The Early Years Foundation Stage framework (DfE, 2012) defines creating and thinking critically as the process whereby 'children have and develop their own ideas, make links between ideas, and develop strategies for doing things' (DfE, 2012: 10). Critical thinking requires skills such as careful observation, analysis and reflecting on ideas. Chatfield states, rigorous critical thinking means not only explaining why we believe something to be the case, but also being obliged to change our minds when our knowledge about the world changes. In this sense, it is related to a purpose that it shares with all scientific and philosophical investigations: searching for the best account we can currently offer of the way things actually are.

(Chatfield, 2018: 15)

Time can be given to enable children to think about why things happen and to ask questions such as 'Why does that happen? What if…?' The child may reflect about an area of learning, an object, an event or an area within the environment.

Case study

A child noticed a growing tree as it changed through the seasons and delighted in the growing leaves and later their shifting autumnal colour. He asked 'Why have the leaves fallen from the trees? What makes this happen? Will it affect other things?' He asked his friends. One wondered if it was someone called Jack Frost, whom he'd heard about, who had taken the leaves, and observed 'Look, he's stashed them in the corner.' The boy watched as the leaves swirled around. He saw them blowing and falling from trees nearby. An adult questioned him about the changing seasons and he remembered when he'd visited the park one hot, sunny day in the summer. 'It's autumn now,' he said, 'and it'll be getting colder in winter.' He kicked the fallen leaves, listening to them crunch underfoot, then entered the setting and took a book about autumn that was on display, noting pictures of trees in autumn.

Other observations the children might make could concern the space and suggestions for improvements or additions to go with a current theme. This could for example involve taking turns in the role play or painting area, or suggestions for changing the layout, such as one young girl's idea: 'Could we have somewhere that is really quiet so we can read and think?' This may be something the adults had realised and may be a positive addition for the provision. In the case of the additional 'very quiet' space in the setting, this was arranged and proved very effective for children's reflective practice. The independent activities and free flow of opportunities in an early years learning environment lends itself to philosophical questions that the children might have and to their pondering about the world around them: for example, 'Why does time go slow sometimes?' or 'What makes someone a best friend?'

Children's voice

As a child growing up in the mid-20th century is was not uncommon to hear the retort 'Children should be seen and not heard,' with expectations that we, as children, would sit and listen to our elders and betters when we met others and would not speak. In settings in the 21st century it is usual to hear a merry buzz of children's chatter as they engage in their activities and observe that they have also been part of such tasks as designing the setting rules for those who access the provision and the themes that are explored within it. This practice begins at the earliest moments for the child, with interactions between parent or carer and baby, and two-way non-verbal communication. As children's confidence and language proficiency grows this can be encouraged and developed as they enter new provision facilities. Listening to a range of views from different perspectives, a holistic understanding of the child can be gained. Children's voice, however, does not mean a noisy outburst when inappropriate; rather it connotes thoughtful contributions to discussions, demonstrating respect for others. Further knowledge about an individual can be garnered through a mosaic approach to providing children's activities, with a variety of activities – painting, drawing, mark-making, construction work, physical actions, music and language – laid on. Such activities may provide deep insights into a child's thoughts, for example a painting can reflect how a child feels or can recount an experience. The key person can promote children's voice through their knowledge of the child and through an understanding of appropriate strategies to encourage children to voice opinions and thoughts in an atmosphere where their views will be valued.

Another reason for adults to listen carefully to children's ideas is that children may be attempting to describe an incident that has happened to them but that appears unusual in your understanding of them.

Case study

In a British setting with an ethnically diverse group of children a child with an African first name explained to an adult that he had always lived in the UK and was born here. This was disbelieved by the key person, as she felt she knew his family and background and that the child must be confused. At the end of the year a party was arranged and the adult told him he could come in his national dress if he liked, as many of his friends were coming in the national dress of the place where they were born. His elder sister claimed the national dress must be jeans and a t-shirt in the part of London where her brother was born.

Reflections

What are your thoughts about children's voice?
How do you reflect these thoughts in your practice with young children?

The UN Convention on the Rights of the Child and the Children Act 1989

The Children Act (1989) highlights aspects significant for creating and critical thinking. This includes the values of self-esteem and resilience, which are recognised as essential to every child's development. 'Children not only need to feel that they are loved and secure but also that they are respected and accepted by adults outside the family. Having a good level of self-esteem enables children to cope with criticism and negative comments about themselves' (Curtis and O'Hagan, 2009: 5). Resilience is linked to self-esteem and this would be reflected in children's contributions to discussions where there are views that differ from the child's own. According to Curtis and O'Hagan the Children's Act 'ensured that the welfare of the child was paramount and allowed children's opinions to be taken into account' (2009: 19).

Activities to promote thinking skills

Moylett and Stewart (2012) suggest in *Development Matters* that creating and critical thinking for early years children covers having your own ideas, making links and choosing ways to do things. Children having their own ideas consists of generating new suggestions, finding ways to solve problems and finding new ways to do things. Making links includes making connections and noticing patterns in their experience, making predictions, testing their ideas and developing ideas about grouping, sequences, cause and effect. Choosing ways to do things incorporates planning, making decisions about how to approach a task, solve a problem and reach a goal, checking how well their activities are going, changing strategy as needed and reviewing how well the approach worked. Children are able to make connections and enhance understanding.

Stimulus materials can foster philosophical critical thinking, for example with the use of stories to stimulate discussion of notions of right or wrong based on the behaviour of characters and events within the story. This could be followed by an activity such as 'hot-seating,' where a child assumes a character and other children ask him or her questions, with the child responding in the guise of the character. In that way children can listen to other points of view and gain insights into others' perspectives on situations, challenging and questioning each other and reconstructing their own views. Circle time issues, for example discussions about bullying, are also a useful way to gain insights into differing views and understanding about how a child feels. A circle focus in a setting concerned 'talking about myself.' A child who had difficulties participating in activities with his peers spoke about how he felt at home being brought up by his grandparents while his single parent dad was absent. The four-year-olds in the group immediately understood, without prompting by the adult, and demonstrated empathy and support for the child.

The IAPC suggests ways in which participants in discussions can consider their position throughout the meeting, as follows:

- Have we begun to deal with the question?
- What do we understand now about the question/concept that we didn't understand before?
- Are we giving each other reasons for our views?
- Are we listening to each other?
- Are we able to stick to the point?
- Are we able to build on each other's ideas?
- Who is doing the talking?
- Do we correct each other with sensitivity?
- Are we becoming more tentative about what we claim to know?
- Do we trust each other?

The independence of the early years environment provides a rich atmosphere to promote thinking, contrasting with more formal approaches where children may be confined to specific set lessons and lack time to reflect on issues during the school day. Reflections in such a formal context may be confined to the designated subject matter until the daily demands of school are completed.

Child-centred, child-initiated learning conversely flows readily into opportunities for philosophical considerations. These approaches are linked to theoretical perspectives such as that of Piaget (see Chapter 6), who devised schemas describing how children assimilate and accommodate experiences and information in their activities and within their contexts.

Language development

Language acquisition is vital to secure children's knowledge of language mores and to cultivate sufficient language understanding to appreciate what is being said. Chomsky's

(1928–) theory of the Language Acquisition Device (LAD) suggested children have an instinctive ability to access language understanding. His theory asserts that children are born with an innate facility to develop language. The nativist theory proposed by Chomsky stated that the brain operates universal syntactic rules applicable to all languages. However, particular synapses in the brain strengthen with stimuli: individual languages stress different sounds, the processing of which is thus reinforced in the individual brain, occasionally leading to some difficulties when hearing certain unfamiliar intonations (e.g. from other languages). The experience of Genie, a child left alone and neglected, demonstrated that she was unable to speak in sentences when rehabilitated, despite expert support and care. The behaviourist theory proposed by Skinner, contra Chomsky, claimed that language was learnt through operant conditioning, with children gaining positive feedback through appropriate language responses.

Vygotsky and Bruner highlighted the importance of interactions to promote language acquisition. They emphasised the importance of children's interactions with peers and adults as a means to develop thinking skills and concepts through language and communication with others. Bruner's social-interactionist theory proposed a Language Acquisition Support System (LASS): children in an early years setting will be developing their listening abilities. Development from non-verbal communication to understanding of words and sentences varies in rate. Some young children may be at a one-word level of understanding when they access a setting. Adults would need to appreciate this and respond accordingly to a child's understanding, while helping the child to remember increasingly complex language constructions.

Contributions and participation in discussions of philosophical issues can promote a feeling of self-esteem and confidence as they give children an opportunity to argue about a situation and feel secure in their judgement as to its appropriateness. Such a process fosters trust in others, whether they agree of not, in that they are sufficiently confident in the relationship to share inner thoughts with others and know that those ideas will be treated with respect and valued irrespective of whether there is agreement. The National Curriculum (DfEE/QCA, 1999) identifies five elements of thinking skills, namely information processing, reasoning, enquiry, creative thinking and evaluation. In 2001, Wallace first published Thinking Actively in a Social Context (TASC – Wallace et al., 2012), a resource used to identify and develop thinking skills. The incorporation of thinking skills and a philosophical approach appears to be gaining popularity among early years and school frameworks. Marsden (2012: 110), through action research in a school where she was head teacher, found that introducing sessions based on philosophical discussions had a significant impact on children's confidence and thinking skills.

BLOOM'S TAXONOMY

The adult facilitator

The adult facilitator has the responsibility for providing a welcoming environment where the child, parent or carer will feel at ease and sufficiently appreciated to be confident in speaking to the adults working there. The layout of the setting, displays, reading material available, resources and activities planned may all give clues as to the extent of the welcome. Non-verbal communication, such as a welcoming smile or eye contact, can play a significant part in ensuring relationships can be developed to secure a strong partnership. Consideration should be given to whether any particular provision required for the child, such as a wider space between equipment or access at an appropriate level, has been addressed. Understandings of how confident they feel in the setting can be gained by questions to learn about how they are responding to the facility, such as what area they like to use or who they like to play with.

Children receive strong messages about their worth through their interactions with others. In discussions they will respond to verbal and non-verbal communication. If this is negative it can damage their self-esteem and feelings of self-worth, impacting on their ability to participate in discussions or voice their opinions. Sometimes children may be extremely quiet in a setting, lacking in confidence to speak, while at home parents note the child has become very noisy, possibly as a backlash against repression and a mismatch among expectations. Meaningful continuities of experience are crucial in ensuring children feel secure during transition times.

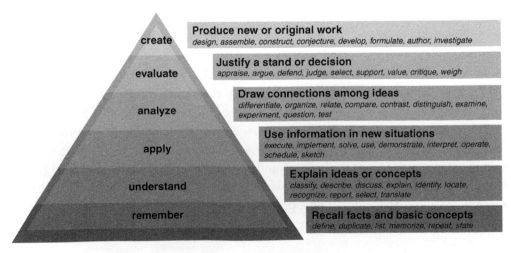

Figure 5.1 Bloom's taxonomy

Sourced and adapted from Vanderbilt University Centre for Teaching (n.d.)

The adult facilitates the discussions and questioning in a myriad of ways. Facilitation may take the form of an informal interaction with a child or children, as in the first case study in the chapter (see p. 81), or may involve a group or whole-class discussion where the facilitator encourages the children to devise, with him or her, a set of guidelines to promote effective discussion, for example listening to others, showing respect for others' views, letting anyone in the group speak or taking turns to speak. The adult may encourage the speakers and suggest questions which scaffold the responses and deepen the understanding of the issue and different viewpoints on it. Strategies can be employed to encourage a variety of responses, such as individual work, paired discussions and discussions in groups or with the whole class. Where the conversations take place can have an impact on what is said. Children will differ in where they are most communicative and at ease. A child visiting another space next to his familiar area was initially unable to speak until he felt sufficiently secure to voice his thoughts. Some may prefer speaking while they are busy working on practical activities while others may prefer a discussion around a table or in a circle of chairs. There are a number of ways the adult can deliver talk to children. Adults could use rote communication, giving facts through routines and repetition; recitation, using short question/answer sequences to recall what is expected to be known already; instruction, telling children what to do and how to do it; exposition, imparting information and explaining things; and – crucially for the development of thinking skills – discussion and scaffolding dialogue.

Discussion and scaffolding

Discussion entails the open exchange of views and information in order to explore issues and consider ideas and the resolution of problems. Scaffolded dialogue encourages children to think, and to think in different ways. It promotes responses to questions which require much more than simple recall. The answers given can be followed up and built on rather than merely received. It ensures feedback, which can provide information and leads thinking forward. The contributions can be extended, rather than gaining a fragmented response through one-word replies. The scaffolded exchanges link together to form a coherent whole, which develops knowledge and understanding and deepens enquiry and insights. The environment fosters an atmosphere of trust and values all as individuals with strong relationships – almost a bonding of outlook. This form of dynamic talk and these kinds of relationships can contribute to the development of those participating: one person can develop the capacity to respond to and take forward the views of others. Scaffolding can provide peers with an appropriate linguistic foundation to bridge the gap between present and further understanding. Handover can take place, with a successful transfer of what is to be learned and new learning assimilated to existing knowledge and understanding. Discussion and dialogue require learners not merely to listen and answer, but also to think, engage and take decisions about their learning. By using discussion and dialogue learners are empowered both cognitively and socially, not merely told things or checked to see what they already know.

Questioning

Questioning can actively promote children's thinking and encourage their consideration of issues. Capacities to understand, apply, analyse, evaluate, create and remember can be fostered through adult/child discussions. During activities children can be encouraged to narrate what they are doing, explain, analyse what they have found, speculate about what might have happened, explore reasons, evaluate them, discuss their findings with others, argue with respect, justify their opinions and ask questions of their own. In learning, as in life, the forms of talk are important. To facilitate the different types of learning talk children can be encouraged to listen to others, think about what they hear, give others time to think and respect alternative viewpoints.

Effective listening

Interactions between babies and young children and their parent, carer or key person are the foundations for promoting critical thinking. It is important for adults to concentrate on their listening when communicating with the child. Despite the appearance of listening, if the adult is concentrating on something else the child will be aware of this, resulting in impaired responses and damaging the child's self-esteem. The interactions should be a two-way process to scaffold learning, a situation referred to as sustained shared thinking. This shared thinking could occur between a child or an adult, or child and child, or as group members collaborate. Adults can model the process, particularly in a new situation or with a new resource input. Care should be taken to allow children to develop their own ideas rather than copying the model demonstrated.

Reflections

Are you able to structure questions from easily answered closed questions to open ended ones?

If you have used this style of questioning, what did you notice about the child's response? Was it a reflective answer as the open, probing questions developed?

If you are a practitioner with a larger group of children do you ensure everyone has the opportunity to respond to questions?

Do you give them time to reflect on their responses?

How do you encourage those more hesitant to respond?

In what ways do you encourage those who like constantly to speak above others to listen to their peers?

Enabling environments

The ethos of the environment should value children's ideas and allow time for them to design and attempt them with a variety of materials. Routines can be flexible yet within structure to allow children to feel secure. Thinking can be presented in different ways, for example as a large 'thought shower' drawn together or as a table-top visual diagram. Achievements can be celebrated for how they have been accomplished and the process used, not just the outcome. Babies and toddlers can be given space and resources to explore. These can be carefully stored so as to accommodate them in a small setting yet remain stimulating and readily available for use.

Provision for older children will require careful design, organisation and cooperative management to ensure resources are fully utilised, readily available and adequately stored so that children can access them.

Multiple intelligences

Gardner (1983) suggested that individual young children and adults have preferred learning styles. The implications for early years practitioners were that they should cater for these different styles, including linguistic, musical, logical-mathematical, spatial, bodily kinaesthetic, intrapersonal intelligence, interpersonal intelligence and naturalistic intelligence. These are catered for in most early years settings, if not all, as part of the daily free-flow activities. It can be observed how some children enjoy working continually in one way, for example outdoors, painting, or at the woodwork table or mark-marking area. Children can be encouraged to attempt all areas to develop skills in others aspects of the framework and to avoid becoming afraid to try something new. They can also be encouraged to develop their skills in their preferred aspect to enhance this area and possibly use it as a springboard into other ones.

Gardner's multiple intelligences concept demonstrates that all areas of the framework can benefit from deep, insightful questioning and thinking skills approaches so that children can gain the most from their experiences. The Williams Report (Williams, 2008) strongly endorsed the findings of the Effective Provision of Pre-School Education project (EPPE), which highlighted the importance of the early years in children's development and the lasting effects these years have. The report stated,

> Central to effective mathematical pedagogy in the early years is fostering children's natural interest in numeracy, problem solving, reasoning, shapes and measures. Children should be given opportunities in a broad range of contexts, both indoors and outdoors, to explore, enjoy, learn, practise and talk about their developing mathematical understanding. Vitally important is ensuring that children's mathematical experiences are fun, meaningful and build confidence.
>
> (Williams, 2008: 34)

The report emphasises the importance of open-ended discussions about solutions, the exploration of reasoning and mathematical logic.

> ### Reflections
>
> *Do you have a preferred way of learning?*
> *Have you noticed one of the children in your care has a specific gift or talent in one area?*

Values

Values are increasingly incorporated into settings as part of a holistic approach to children's learning. This incorporation is a principle that guides critical thinking and, in turn, behaviour and the rationale for it. Children develop a sense of self and trust in relationships. They can reflect on their learning and their experiences. Children's reflection can concern many values: they can express views on emotions or ways of behaving and thinking (for example, thoughtfulness, love, happiness, caring, hope, peace, co-operation or tolerance). This can be linked to an overarching approach, such as one employing music to encourage thoughtfulness, and a whole setting or school focus, so that everyone can be involved in the discussions, including through home/setting partnerships. It can be introduced through a variety of strategies such as hot seating or freeze frames. It can empower children to begin to overcome their own problems or challenges and helps them empathise with and respect others. The learning environment is enhanced through the underpinning holistic values. Incorporating values contributes to the personal development of each child and adult involved, as part of a changing social community.

When the child is allowed to think for themselves, knows how to analyse and consider happenings and the views of others and has the capacity to attempt an idea, evaluate it and be sufficiently resilient to learn from mistakes, he or she can learn and become confident in the world.

References

Chatfield, T. (2018) *Critical Thinking* London: Sage
Curtis, A. O'Hagan, M. (2009) *Care and Education in Early Childhood* London: Routledge
Department for Education (2012) *The Early Years Foundation Stage Framework* London: DfE
Department for Education and Employment with Qualifications and Curriculum Authority (DfEE/ QCA) (1999) *The National Curriculum: Handbook for Primary Teachers in England* London: DfEE
Gardner, H. (1983) *Frames of Mind: The Theory of Multiple Intelligences* New York: Basic Books

Institute for the Advancement of Philosophy for Children (IAPC) (n.d.) What is Philosophy for Children Montclair State University, College of Education and Human Services https://www.montclair.edu/cehs/academics/centers-and-institutes/iapc/what-is/

Marsden, S. (2012) Thinking skills in Beckley, P. (Ed.) *Learning in Early Childhood* London: Sage

Moylett, H. Stewart, N. (2012) *Development Matters* London: Early Education/DfE – The British Association for Early Childhood Education

Vanderbilt University Center for Teaching (n.d.) Bloom's Taxonomy https://cft.vanderbilt.edu/guides-sub-pages/blooms-taxonomy/

Wallace, B. Bernardelli, A. Molyneux, C. (2012) TASC: Thinking Actively in a Social Context. A universal problem-solving process *Gifted International Journal* 28(1) 58–83

Williams, P. (2008) *Independent Review of Mathematics Teaching in Early Years Settings and Primary Schools* London: Department for Children, Schools and Families

Perspectives on learning
A changing environment

Pat Beckley

Overview

The chapter considers perspectives on learning and how these can influence what is taught and how it is delivered. The views of key theorists, namely Rousseau, Piaget, Vygotsky, Skinner and Bruner, will be discussed, along with how they impact upon approaches used. Different learning environments will be explored along with a possible rationale concerning why they should be different. The effect of the international view of early years learning will be considered in terms of sharing ideas and converging practice through placing specific elements in different and changing contexts.

Introduction

There are different perspectives on learning, with interactions and communication between those involved in early years helping such practitioners to devise their own strategies and approaches that fit their preferred philosophies. A chosen philosophy could entail a focus on the child as unique and developing at his or her own pace. An early years philosophy could also (or alternatively) view early years as a means of introducing the child to society's mores and ways of working, where the child is required to fit a pre-determined set of targets. However, Waller suggests (2005: 59) that 'there are multiple and diverse childhoods and in order to study childhood one has to consider a range of perspectives.'

To briefly overview a selection of perspectives: *nativism* stems from the belief that a child has innate capabilities and that children learn from an appropriate environment. *Empiricism* incorporates the notion of a child being rather passive in their learning, with a professional delivering the appropriately devised learning environment. Such a philosophy can accommodate an *instructivist* approach, with an emphasis on 'preparing for school...aiming for equality of educational opportunity and the means to improve later education.' This approach is taken where childhood services for children aged 3–6 are seen as an initial stage of schooling (McQuail et al., 2003: 14). *Instructivism* argues that children should be instructed in predetermined facts to enable them to progress in their learning. In a *constructivist*

approach early childhood is seen as a stage in its own right, with children viewed as competent learners and co-constructors of their learning.

Constructivism

> acknowledges that children are born with cognitive capabilities and potential, and sees each child constructing knowledge and developing through cognitive activity in interaction with his or her environment. Children create their own meaning and understanding, combining what they already know and believe to be true with new experiences.

> (Woods, 1998)

Social constructivist views emphasise the need for children to use social interactions with their peers and adults to formulate constructions of the world and develop their concepts.

The adoption and pursuit of one of these philosophical approaches to learning in the early years has major implications for the way the child is treated and for communications between the adult and child and between children. Through a strategy devised according to the adult's beliefs a child gains an understanding of the world that surrounds them. Children respond to the world around them as a reflection of experiences they have in the family or with those close to them, as well as with the local community and the wider world.

Approaches in England, Norway and Uganda

Early years policies in England, Norway and Uganda all have an emphasis on literacy as a core skill, crucial in the modern world. However, a different approach is apparent in each country as to how this can be achieved. Differing historical and cultural perspectives, economic forces and political agendas impact on the way literacy is taught and the approaches used to deliver the elements of literacy teaching and learning. In England a stimulating environment with numerous resources, along with structured programmes such as phonics planning, support children's knowledge of communication and language as a 'prime area of learning and development' in the early years foundation stage (EYFS) framework, with literacy a specific area to be covered. This is usually delivered in a classroom environment, with walls richly covered with interactive displays and a use of indoor and outdoor space. In Norway, language is also deemed highly important as a factor for literacy. This is incorporated into interactions through a largely outdoor experience where young children can learn about their world and enjoy story-telling through the natural, outdoor environment. In Uganda the classrooms contain desks and chairs to enable the children to learn the English words displayed on the blackboard. Interactions through chants and praise for individual children attempting new learning enable children to become highly proficient at writing skills. These ways of delivering the teaching and learning of literacy appear very different, due to their foundations in the cultures in which they belong. In England, coverage of the guidelines is important; this frames the work planned in the long term to influence what is taught in a shorter period. The practitioner can be relatively flexible about how this is delivered, in line with the philosophy of the school culture. Responses to governmental initiatives are important and specific training can be given for aspects required. In Norway the attachment to nature is evident in the children's play. Besides learning how to use materials to make, for example, dens, they learn to use the cold weather to their advantage, such as by making snow shelters, to promote their independence and knowledge of how to respond to sudden Arctic conditions – as well as enjoying their beautiful surroundings. Uganda is a developing country which is progressing rapidly, and the national 'Education for All' policy reflects a desire to have a skilled workforce to drive future advancement. In the community visited some families chose which child in the family to support in their learning through funds for school uniforms and necessary books. This is reflected in the delivery of the sessions, where children are instructed to ensure they cover such areas as language and mathematical skills through written practise and activities to promote health. The healthy development of all children was apparent in England, Norway and Uganda, with daily exercises in England, often to music, outdoor activities in Norway and physical games and activities in Uganda.

These different philosophical approaches to learning and teaching are based on various theoretical bases, and implemented through the beliefs and values of the practitioners working with the young children.

Rousseau (1712–78)

Jean-Jacques Rousseau was born in Geneva and become an influential philosopher. His mother died a few days after his birth and he was raised by his father, who led him to appreciate written works and nature. Rousseau met a seamstress and had children with her whom he gave to an orphanage, claiming he did not have the means to support them. However, he later wrote key works which influenced thinking concerning how to bring up children, and which are relevant in the modern world. Rousseau thought children were born pure and that society marred their understanding of such aspects as morality and right and wrong, a view which was relatively controversial during his lifetime. This gave rise to a theory emphasising the importance of nature, where children could independently learn by exploring their surroundings and finding out about them. Rousseau considered the role of the adult to be that of a facilitator for the child; one who observes the child, assesses them and interacts to encourage discovery of further knowledge. Rousseau divided development into three stages. Initially children are guided by their emotions and impulses until the age of 12. They begin to reason from 12 to 16. After this children begin to develop into adults. This philosophical stance bears comparison with similar ideas that feature in current practice. However, Rousseau believed that women should follow a man's lead and be occupied with domestic activities.

Piaget (1896–1980)

Jean Piaget believed that children build their knowledge by passing through a number of stages, each developing from the previous stage. His view is known as constructivism, because children construct their learning as they build on their experiences and make sense of them through their own understandings. He felt that children should pass through four cognitive stages and should assimilate each stage before passing to the next. The stages he defined were the sensorimotor stage (birth–2 years); pre-operational stage (2–7 years); concrete operational stage (7–11 years); and formal operational stage (11 years upwards).

Piaget used the terms *assimilation* and *accommodation* to explain the processes happening during the stages. Assimilation concerns how perceptions and adaptations of new information are fitted into pre-existing schemas. Accommodation occurs when existing schemas are changed to fit new information.

Sensorimotor stage (birth–2 years)

Piaget divided the sensorimotor stage into six sub-divisions. These consisted of (i) simple reflexes; (ii) first habits and a primary circular reactions phase; (iii) a secondary reactions phase; (iv) a coordination of secondary circular reactions stages; (v) a tertiary circular reactions, novelty and curiosity stage; and finally (vi) internalisation of schemas.

Pre-operational stage (2–7 years)

During this stage children are still egocentric and have difficulty considering the views of others. Children are at a symbolic function substage and can recall objects and picture objects without their being in front of them. This phase also comprises the concurrent intuitive thought substage, when children want to know about everything around them and frequently ask questions such as 'Why?' or 'How come?' Children can think in images and symbols. They can participate in role play and social activities.

Concrete operational stage (7–11)

This stage follows the preoperational stage and the child has the ability to use logic, for example to solve problems based on concrete objects. Piaget claimed that children can use inductive reasoning. This entails deriving inferences from observations to make generalisations. During this stage they increasingly become aware of their own uniqueness and devise plans to solve problems. They are aware of who they are in social matters and consider what future they might have.

Formal operational stage (11 onwards)

Young people are able to use symbols related to abstract concepts during this stage. They are able to consider 'what-if' situations, a capacity which Piaget termed 'hypothetico-deductive reasoning.' Concrete thought processes are replaced by the capacity for abstract thought. Individuals in this stage are capable of problem solving and have meta-cognition, the ability to think about thinking.

Reflections

What are the strengths in Piaget's ideas?
Can you think of any weaknesses in Piaget's proposals?

While Piaget considered a growing knowledge of the world around the child and their conceptual understanding of it, his theory did not acknowledge social and cultural factors or the differences between individual children. This could have problems in practice, for example if a practitioner does not want a child to attempt activities which may be part of the next step as they believe the child will not be 'ready.' In one example, a practitioner did not want to let a child have access to a reading scheme book as the child was unable to read a word out of context. She believed the child was 'not ready.' It also has implications for 'school readiness' where it is felt a child has not attained specific skills necessary for school, while it could be suggested conversely that the school should adjust its practice to suit the needs of the child.

Vygotsky (1896–1934)

Lev Vygotsky was a developmental psychologist and introduced the notion of the 'zone of proximal development' (ZPD), as well as identifying the importance of play in children's learning. He organised child development in three levels (see Figure 6.1), with the initial level based on a child's independent learning, followed by interactions with

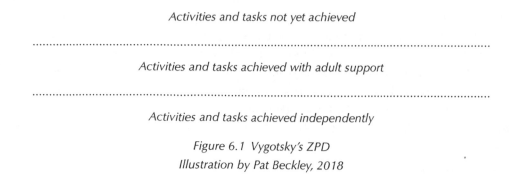

Activities and tasks not yet achieved

....

Activities and tasks achieved with adult support

....

Activities and tasks achieved independently

Figure 6.1 Vygotsky's ZPD
Illustration by Pat Beckley, 2018

an adult who can promote a child's learning, and an upper level of potential skill that a child could reach following input.

Vygotsky's zone of proximal development

Vygotsky highlighted the significance of cultural mediation and interpersonal communication in learning in order to achieve higher mental functions. He felt that there was a strong link between inner speech and oral language and the effect this has on mental concepts and cognitive awareness. Inner speech would organise thoughts and develop concepts, a process that would be influenced by social interactions that supported this development. This higher state was achieved through interactions and a shared understanding of culture through internalisation, using activities within society.

Skinner (1904–1990)

B. F. Skinner was influenced by the work of Ivan Pavlov (1849–1936), who observed behaviour in dogs and noticed that when a bell was rung and food appeared, the dogs learnt to associate the ringing of the bell with food. This behaviourist theory was termed *classical conditioning*. Skinner wondered whether behaviour could be observed that was not responding to a reflex action. He termed such conditional behaviour *operant conditioning*. He used reinforcements to programme behaviour. These reinforcements were changed – for example to negative, positive or intermittent reinforcement – to observe what differences this made to behaviour.

Bruner (1915–2016)

Jerome Bruner's constructivist theory concerns three representations of development. The *enactive representation* taking place between birth and a year old involves storing action-based information in the memory, for example beating a drum. This muscle memory can be found too in later life, such as in playing a tune on an instrument as a result of repeated practise. *Iconic representation* occurs from 1–6 years and involves remembering information in the form of images. In later life it may be easier to remember information if it includes pictorial presentations or diagrams. *Symbolic representation* occurs from 7 years onwards. Knowledge can be stored and remembered in symbolic forms. Bruner believed a child is able to learn complex ideas via a spiral curriculum, through discovery learning and language interactions with those around them. In Bruner's conception this is a continuous process, not a series of stages. Bruner's proposed spiral curriculum involved revisiting subjects many times but at increasingly complex levels. He felt learning would be promoted through a social interactionist perspective on scaffolded learning, where children communicate to develop their understanding. This begins at the earliest age when children observe, listen and respond to communication and the language of others, a process supported through a cognitive Language Acquisition Support System (LASS).

Philosophy into practice

In this section the legacy of the theories of Rousseau, Piaget, Vygotsky and Bruner are considered in the light of current approaches and ideas concerning early years learning.

Rousseau

Rousseau's ideas link closely with those settings which use exploration as a basis for learning. Resources can be made available to facilitate children's independent development of understanding through observation and their own interests. The love of nature as a means to gain knowledge and understanding also has resonance with many settings' current philosophy. The role of the adult as a facilitator of this knowledge is a way of promoting children's learning that concords with present notions of how babies and young children develop concepts.

Piaget

Piaget emphasised the importance of children reflecting, assimilating and accommodating independently to form schemas about the world. Adults working with the children are able to assess where children are in the stages given, provide tasks and activities for them and know that they will help them to progress to the next stage. These are apparent in children's independent play where they are able to attempt activities and think about what is happening. This corresponds to the cultivation of concepts of thinking. Piaget felt that children should experience tasks at their appropriate level of attainment and stage within his theoretical framework. The importance of the process of learning was highlighted to give children time to think about what is happening around them.

Vygotsky

Vygotsky's theoretical articulation of the zone of proximal development resonates for current practice whereby adults track and assess the stage of development the child has achieved and plan strategies to build on this, through activities and interactions between the adult and child that promote higher levels of learning. The model emphasises the importance of interactions with peers and adults to enhance independent learning and reach higher levels of understanding. The diverse nature of children's and adults' backgrounds would help to provide a wider range of experiences and opportunities to share different views and understandings.

Skinner

Skinner's behaviourist theory has influenced strategies in environments for young children where a set of behaviours is desired and rewards and punishments given in response to evidence of the behaviours. This gains a swift response from children who will eagerly await a star, sticker or other treat, or may desire further attention even with a negative response. It could ultimately secure a response from the child simply to please the adult or gain a prize, rather than considering the rights and wrongs of a situation and self- regulating behaviour.

Bruner

Bruner devised a 'scaffold' as a way of supporting the child's learning. A scaffold could be used in the development of knowledge about an object or subject, or across a series of lessons to gain understanding of an area of learning. It could also involve the whole school in a project covering the same subject area, with each age phase undertaking an aspect of the project appropriate to the development and attainment of the children, gradually becoming more complex as the children grew in their awareness. Children can learn through discovery and careful monitoring and assessment can support their progress. Language interactions are particularly important to promote thinking and can be incorporated into teaching and learning in a variety of ways. Parental involvement and gaining an understanding of children's backgrounds, to use as a rich source of experience, would also be incorporated in the child's learning, for example through home/school collaboration with activities.

Case study

A school decided to use Bruner's spiral curriculum and staff worked together to devise activities as a basis for children's discovery learning. It was agreed to use the environment as a focus for the whole-school project. Younger children considered their immediate environment and studied plant growth, using their vegetable and flower garden as a starting point to observe and experiment. Minibeasts, including in the nearby pond, were observed and growth monitored. Older children considered the locality and visited the garden centre, working with staff to design gardens and plant their school plots to further develop their work. Older children discussed sustainability, the food chain and layers of vegetation, visiting the local horticultural college to gain more information from the students and staff there. Children liaised with interested parents, carers and grandparents, gardeners, park staff and those rearing creatures such as butterflies or chicks. All the children in the school devised ways to sustain the school environment and gave ideas such as a tidy rota for clearing outdoor pathways, which greatly enhanced their understanding of sustainability issues on a wider scale.

Discussions between pairs, groups, the whole class and team phases occurred throughout the project and home/school activities reinforced the interest from the community. Finally school assemblies shared findings from each class with the rest of the school and family members who wished to participate.

Reflections

What aspects of the theories of Rousseau, Piaget, Vygotsky, Skinner and Bruner do you agree with?
In what ways do they differ?
How have the theories or aspects of the theories impacted on your work with babies and young children? How have you considered different representations of stages of development for children as they get older?
How do you promote children's interactions with their peers and adults?

Learning and teaching

There are myriad views about what constitutes learning and teaching. Those who were in schools in the early 1990s may remember 'literacy clocks,' used when teachers were encouraged to give key information at specific times during the daily literacy hour, a technique that often seeped into early years provision to accommodate concerns about the forthcoming SATs in Year 2. Teaching could be seen as a means for an adult to formally pour out information to fill children's waiting brains, or, as discussed in the theoretical section, as a way of facilitating understandings and concepts through exploration and discovery, where the adult secures resources and objects to encourage this at an appropriate level of attainment for the child. In similar terms learning could be viewed as a memorisation of facts, or as 'deep learning,' a thorough understanding of happenings. Where does school readiness fit with these notions? Dewey (1859–1952) argued that education and learning are social and interactive processes. He believed the school is a social institution and that students should interact with the curriculum and have the opportunity to take part in their own learning. In *The Child and the Curriculum* (1902) Dewey discussed the two major differences in educational standpoints as described earlier. He argued that students must be able to relate their learning to their experiences, building on new knowledge. He also debated whether education was too child-centred, claiming that learning should be exploratory within a learning process, for example as in the current problem-based learning activities where children are given a problem to consider and explore possible solutions themselves, ensuring their learning is deepening, consolidating and progressing.

Education for all

Should everyone be given the same education as others? At first it seems logical that we should all have the same opportunities, but what does that entail? The theories explored in this chapter indicate the need to treat children as individuals with different needs. Maslow's hierarchy of needs theory, articulated in his 1943 paper 'A Theory of Human Motivation', identified that children had a physiological need for food and clothing at a basic level, so strategies would need to be in place to support those requiring this aspect before they are able to learn, with for example the provision of a breakfast club. Development through national frameworks would also depend on a child's progress on an individual level; as a Norwegian colleague told me, 'Every child is good at something,' so all have something to offer – although the strengths of each may lie in different aspects.

Those involved with young children may need to reflect upon their personal and cultural views with a degree of insightful honesty, as often these are so deep that it is difficult to appreciate them until another set of values or cultural mores is evident. Care needs to be taken with such aspects as gender equality, to ensure all children have access to resources and are not affected when attempting all activities by possible negative verbalised or non-verbalised views held by adults. Incentives such as rewards can be monitored to ensure fair distribution that demonstrates the strengths each child has.

Two-year-old health and development review

Those identified as requiring further support may have been identified at birth or as they grow. The two-year-old check may identify some issues but many conditions appear when a child is a little older, for example asthma or diabetes. Strategies can be put in place to support individual needs as part of the ethos that olds every child to be unique and with personal strengths to be celebrated. The two-year health and development review provides an opportunity to share any concerns among parents or carers and health services. Advice and information is available for issues such as toilet training or sleep management; the review is also an opportunity to discuss early years education and offer guidance, for example on behaviour strategies.

A cycle of observations, planning, reflections, actions for change, planning, implementing, observations of improvements etc. can be used to form a continuous, on-going rationale for change and for identifying activities to be implemented.

Early years learning and teaching

There is much debate about what constitutes high-quality early learning and teaching. European guidelines aim to support practitioners in their planning, with resources and with the practice of delivery: an example guideline is the European Commission's (1996) ten-year plan for *Quality Targets in Services for Young Children*. As demonstrated in earlier discussions concerning the learning and teaching in England, Norway and Uganda, although policies may appear similar, implementation in context may be different. Constraints may include such factors as numbers in the provision, financial concerns, space available, staffing, resources or ages of children.

Following discussions in the previous section concerning the monitoring and tracking of children's development, we turn now to ongoing formative assessments, which support what is to be prepared for babies and young children to encourage their exploratory behaviour and discoveries. Play-based learning enables ready observations of children's independent and social behaviour by adults around them. Observational assessments can focus on differing aspects as required, whether of the individual child, groups of children, areas of activity or from a specific concern where further information is required to ascertain the next steps for the child. The presence of different children, the need to respond to their interests and the requirement to implement new initiatives deemed relevant by staff mean the setting is constantly evolving. An early focus on children's independent and social behaviour is vital to ensure none of the children are missed in their play, either by other children or adults.

Rousseau, Piaget, Vygotsky and Bruner all highlighted the importance of explora-tory play as a factor in young children's learning, although there were differences in their perceptions of what that entailed. Rousseau valued the love of nature and freedom to learn, Piaget wove development around stages to be passed through in independent play, Vygotsky emphasised social interactions to promote learning while exploring and Bruner noted the importance of social, scaffolded learning where discovery is combined with a spiral curriculum. Play is not always prevalent in the early years, however. In Uganda the high numbers of children per group in a relatively small space limit the opportunities for play. The adults carefully combine more formal teaching with active rhymes, stories and songs to music when the outdoor space is available. Recent improvements in funding have led to the purchase of outdoor equipment and small resources to enable the children to develop gross motor skills in play-based activities. Adults structure the activities carefully to show evidence of progress.

In Norway children are able to access outdoor learning socially and occasionally independently, if they require time to reflect on their learning. Children's independence is encouraged and the teacher is a facilitator for the children, taking a lead from their interests to develop their learning.

Case study

The barnhage, the Norwegian early years setting, had five groups, with each group preparing for outdoor play at the start of the day. One group had had their breakfast outdoors around the camp fire on the top of a hill. The rest of the children were observed by their key workers as they got ready to go outdoors. It was minus 7 degrees Celsius and children would need to wrap up warmly. All the children threw their own all-in-one snowsuits on the floor and jumped on top of them. They quickly fitted in their arms and legs then stood up. They were ready!

One of the groups put on their skis to ski to the nearby field and spend time practising a variety of outdoor activities including sledging, skiing, throwing hoops, dodging obstacles, role play in the trees or branches, building a snow shelter or 'making' lunch. Snack time was outdoors in the snow.

In England most settings have a rich source of resources which the children can access both indoors and outdoors. Play might occur in a range of ways. It could be solitary play, where the child is on his or her own, parallel play, with one child playing alongside another but not interacting, paired play between two children or group play. It could be complex group play where children have set a challenge for themselves to attempt, for example making a den or building a bridge, with roles emerging such as the leader, builder or planner. It is important to assess which type of play a child is using to enable the child to develop. Each type of play has its uses, for example a child may be using solitary play but be new to a setting and observing the other children and adults to become accustomed to how it is organised. However, encouragement to participate may be needed if a child has initial difficulties in joining in. Strategies can be planned to support this work, as highlighted by Vygotsky and Bruner.

In social play children's cognitive and emotional development are promoted. Children can gain a holistic experience, developing understandings of how to share, and can respond to others through the use of voice and non-verbal communication, gaining insights into another's point of view.

Play provides the means to act out and reflect upon events that have happened, whether happy or sad: this is a way of dealing with emotions and organising where they fit into the children's lives. Play incorporating considerations of equality and diversity can promote the ethos of the setting and provide children with wider awareness of the world around them.

A changing environment

Ideas and initiatives converge between practitioners and those involved with early years learning and teaching through networks for sharing ideas. This disseminates to childcare arrangements, disparate settings, schools and policy makers, all of which can change direction in the light of new findings. The early years environment is constantly changing to reflect the changing views of practitioners, parents or carers and policy makers, or in response to other factors such as economic or employment changes. The early years environment has historically responded to changes: it is a constantly evolving facility to which the adults working with young children respond, through their cultural and personal beliefs and values.

References

European Commission Network Proposals for a Ten Year Action Plan (1996) *Quality Targets in Services for Young Children* Toronto: University of Toronto Childcare Resource and Research Unit

Maslow, A. H. (1943) A theory of human motivation *Psychological Review* 50 370–396.

McQuail, S. Mooney, A. Cameron, C. Candappa, M. Moss, P. Petrie, P. (2003) *Early Years and Childcare International Evidence Project* London: Thomas Coram Research Unit, Institute of Education.

Waller, T. (2005) *An Introduction to Early Childhood: A Multidisciplinary Approach* London: Sage.

Woods, D. (1998) *How Children Think and Learn* Oxford: Blackwell Publishers.

Part 3

Philosophical perspectives for creativity

Creativity in an early years foundation stage setting

Emma Revill with Pat Beckley

Overview

This chapter considers philosophical views concerning creativity and how these impact on an early years foundation stage (EYFS) setting. It will explain how creativity forms a foundation for practice throughout learning and teaching and how adults and children work to promote this perspective.

Introduction

Creativity within the curriculum, rather than simply creative development, encompasses the whole of the activities. It concerns new ideas and consideration of different approaches to challenges. Strategies to encourage creating and critical thinking (see Chapter 5) can promote creativity and generate new ways of viewing the activities and resources that are used. Rogers argues that 'the creative process involves imaginative activity, the ability to generate a variety of ideas (productivity), problem-solving (application of knowledge and imagination to a given situation) and the ability to produce an outcome of value and worth' (Rogers quoted in Willan et al., 2005: 109). The outcome may be a marker in a line of progress, towards a completion later. In order to enable creativity, children need to have sufficient self-esteem to be confident in attempting new approaches; they need to value their ideas enough to take them forward and to voice their plans and experiments.

Theoretical perspectives, such as those of Froebel or Rousseau, highlight the importance of encouraging children's creativity as they learn about themselves and to use creativity as a basis for learning. Vygotsky highlighted the importance of play to encourage the development of children's initiatives while enhancing thinking through peer and adult interactions in the zone of proximal development. Bruner's scaffolding of activities in a socio-dialogue context further stimulates children to use their ideas creatively. Creativity can be incorporated throughout the curriculum, either through problem-solving activities, child-initiated tasks and adult-initiated plans such as 'mantle of the expert' in role play or construction tasks, or in abstract ways, for example using the Philosophy for Children model (P4C). During play children may express their ideas, thoughts and plans through available resources, enabling others to reflect and share the individual's cognitive process with a wider audience. An initial idea, perhaps from a previous activity, resource or artefact, may foster excitement and commitment to addressing an idea.

Creativity for life

Bronfenbrenner (1979) suggests children initially learn about the world from those closest to them, then widen their area of influence. With a basis of creativity and support from adults around them, the child can gain an enhanced perception of their world through curious, exploratory creativity. It could be argued that this approach can be used throughout life, for example when seeking a job or changing location, building on previous experiences and devising a new idea creatively. Throughout this process the child responds to others' ideas, assimilating and reflecting on them while including those deemed relevant in the individual's activity. They listen intently and respond to questions. They might work as a group, negotiating and interacting, possibly taking a defined role within the group. Therefore, while addressing their own plans and ideas they are changing and adapting – or not – as a wider range of views are heard. This is part of the foundation of the individual's journey through their personal opportunities and experiences.

Reflections

Consider times when you have used creativity within a situation or as part of everyday life. What did you do? What was the outcome?
Have you observed a child or children's creativity?
What did they do? How did the adult help to enhance their creativity?

Children become absorbed in their work, identifying its importance to themselves, and when totally engaged are hardly aware of happenings around them. This has implications for timings: these must be managed to enable those involved to complete their task or keep it safe for continuation at another time. Open-ended resources, for example 3D shapes to build into a representation of an idea, are more effective than a 'ready-made' representation: for example a farm created from a variety of materials and incorporating many personal design features is preferable to a bought farm which fits a prescribed format. Brett suggests key aspects for practitioners to consider when devising an environment to accommodate creativity, including key questions a practitioner might imagine a child would ask and the opportunities, spaces, time, materials and records to be kept (Brett cited in Reed et al., 2015: 112). Children will be greatly motivated in a stimulating space that impacts upon their creativity. Reference would need to be made to children's needs, as in Maslow's (1943) hierarchy of needs, to determine that they have the requisite sense of wellbeing and security to use creativity. Children's creativity and awareness can be further enhanced through visits, e.g. visits to the setting from artists musicians or others who use creativity as part of their everyday roles. Children can also visit venues such as museums, libraries or galleries to further widen their experiences and supply ideas to build upon. Adults working with the child can model their own creativity to motivate others. Children and adults' 'sustained shared thinking' can further promote ideas and help gain creative responses or use creativity to address a challenge.

Philosophy into practice

Emma Revill, the EYFS Leader at an 'outstanding' provision, shared her thoughts about ongoing strategies to promote planning, teamwork and the areas of learning.

Planning

Planning for literacy and maths in our one-form-entry setting is carried out weekly by the class teacher, based roughly around the current topic of the term – for example, 'Out of this world' or 'Celebrations and good times'. However, enhanced provision planning is carried out daily with the class teacher with learning support assistance. A grid is used which includes all areas of the classroom and discussions are carried out concerning which activities need to be out in the classroom to enhance the children's learning that week. The activities may relate to the overarching theme of the term or to the maths topic that is being taught that week. In addition, when planning the enhanced provision activities are included based around the children's interests, which may not relate to the topic of the term but are still included so that the environment reflects current interests of the children. Furthermore, within the enhanced provision certain children are identified on the chart which are the 'focus children,' meaning the activity is created with them in mind either for their next steps in learning or for a particular interest they have shown.

Teamwork

Teamwork between practitioners, practitioners and pupils, practitioners and parents is a crucial element for the EYFS environment. As a classroom is a very busy place with lots of learning, communication and creativity happening every minute, the practitioners need to ensure lines of communication are open at all times between themselves. In our setting we use an online platform to take observations of every child but these need to be purposeful and we need to ensure that the assessment being carried out is not repeated several times; daily conservations are held to eradicate this. Using our online platform to carry out observations and assessments means that teamwork with parents/carers can also develop, as parents/carers are able to upload their own observations of their child learning at home, which also reflects children's current interests. These observations help to build a bigger picture of each child and can enhance the provision within the classroom. For example, if a child went horse riding this activity can be demonstrated through fiction and non-fiction books within the reading corner. Teamwork also plays an essential part in children's progress: through the online platform practitioners can note what a child's next step is so that parents/carers can work on this at home, providing a school/home relationship.

Areas of learning

The classroom environment is fundamental to the children's learning and progress. In order to promote creativity I believe the environment needs to be engaging, fun, interesting and well-organised. Practitioners can facilitate this within the confines of the setting. Open-ended activities have proven to be the most popular and I believe are the activities that truly reflect the characteristics of effective learning in children. For example, we have adapted the mathematics area of our classroom so that every activity is open ended. One of the activities we always provide is a number of the day, with corresponding activities such as counting, number formation or games, which relate to a theme. We also provide other resources like pens, whiteboards, fabric/wooden numbers, beads etc. and the children carry out their own mathematical investigations. Higher ability children often take their investigations into their current learning, including addition and subtraction while lower ability children investigate counting and number formation.

Creativity in early years practice

The philosophical rationale for the provision, wherever it is located, will decide what is important, and these factors will be highlighted as a team or leader wishes. It could be a profit-making facility where emphasis is on gaining the most for the least outlay; this could affect such aspects as practitioners' pay, resources and space. Another approach could be to reflect the society the provision serves, as discussed in Chapter 1; provision in different countries could highlight differing learning environments. The learning environment provided may be driven by individual children's outcomes or by social awareness, interactions and abilities. Strong teamwork and a well-planned learning environment enable children entering the early years provision to gain non-verbal as well as verbal confirmation that promotes their sense of wellbeing. They are able to respond confidently, knowing they will be listened to as individuals. Partnerships with parents and carers follows existing links with previous settings. Young children will readily become aware of the relationships existing in the setting and the extent of the welcome for themselves and their parents/carers.

Opportunities for creativity

The environment, indoors and outdoors (see Figure 7.1), can encourage children to generate their own ideas for further explorations, through child-initiated or adult-initiated

Figure 7.1 The outdoor area offers opportunities for exploration, role play, investigation, experimentation, sustained shared thinking, active learning and quiet reflection
Photograph by Pat Beckley, 2017

Figure 7.2 Mathematics materials created to promote creativity
Photograph by Pat Beckley, 2017

activities, supported by sustained shared thinking. In this way learning is cross-curricular and contributes to a holistic development. In the setting shown ideas can begin in one area with resources and materials gathered in other areas, for example inspiration from role play outdoors can lead to dance and music on a stage indoors with music and lighting. Children's individual or group achievements can be shared and individual celebrations highlighted, such as birthdays or key events. The Steiner Waldorf early childhood approach states, 'learning gains meaning by its relevance to life and should not be separated from the business of daily living. The learning experience of children under the age of seven therefore is integrated and not subject-based' (International Association for Steiner-Waldorf Early Childhood Education, n.d.). The integration of the activities accessed either through planned themes, immersive themes originating from a question posed, or a theme developing from a child's interests can form the basis of the holistic approach. In the Montessori approach space is provided with the adult supporting the child. In this way the child is able to pursue creativity and intellectual curiosity and to think freely.

Figure 7.3 The reading area provides space to gain further information and time to think
Photograph by Pat Beckley, 2017

Creativity in resourcing

In this area the adult has set a specific challenge, which is open-ended to allow for children to attempt it in their own way (Figure 7.2). Children can decide the resources used and level of difficulty chosen. They may begin the activity in a variety of ways, for example consolidating previous learning before attempting more difficult number sentences or working with a friend to share their learning. Children are able to gain reinforcement of words connected with the activity and use mark-making to record their work. Adults can monitor progress through this independent play.

Space to be creative

A quiet space for contemplation of ideas and opportunities to gain further information and build on experiences has been created in the reading area (Figure 7.3). The children have time to readjust their thinking and reflect on their work.

Figure 7.4 An exploration and investigation shed as a resource to record and share thoughts incorporated in the active environment indoors and outdoors

Photograph by Pat Beckley, 2017

Time for creativity

Throughout the setting areas for active involvement and quiet reflection are identified. A child can use the base for such activities as a starter for planning, for recording work, as a means of accessing equipment to further their investigations or to share ideas in a cosy venue (Figure 7.4). Ongoing experiments can be stored for future use.

Celebrating creativity

Here, two four-year-old children have worked together to consider the needs of the creatures they are using as their models (Figure 7.5). The model will be kept for a while to display the thought-provoking work to others, enhancing the sense of personal worth felt by the designers of the work through others' praise.

Creativity can be incorporated throughout the environment of the setting and within any area of the EYFS framework. It involves a variety of skills such as imagination,

Figure 7.5 A model of a home for animals, demonstrating the children's care for other creatures and consideration of their needs while providing a record of achievement
Photograph by Pat Beckley, 2017

commitment, originality, confidence, problem-solving and the ability to create some resolution or product. Imagination may be used in any area of learning, including mathematics, language, physical activities, music, art or dance.

Creativity can be inhibited, for example by formal, rigid instruction, or allowed to flourish. It can develop at different rates throughout a lifespan, depending on circumstances and growth patterns. However, it can also be given opportunities to flourish.

In the next chapter John Stafford explores musical provision in the early years as a means to develop in practice the philosophical creativity approach. This is underpinned by the knowledge and understanding of the importance of music as a way of developing holistically through such aspects as language and communication, interactions with others, listening intently and empathising, learning about rhymes and patterns, dance, and sounds. It is through sounds and music that babies and adults interact with one another.

According to Bernadette Duffy (2006), creativity and imagination in the early years should be encouraged as we are promoting children's ability to explore and comprehend their world and increasing their opportunities to make connections and reach new understandings.

References

Bronfenbrenner, U. (1979) *The Ecology of Human Development: Experiments by Nature and Design* Cambridge MA: Harvard University Press

Duffy, B. (2006) *Supporting Creativity and Imagination in Early Years* Oxford: Oxford University Press

International Association for Steiner-Waldorf Early Childhood Education (n.d.) Waldorf Education www.iaswece.org/waldorf-education

Maslow, A. H. (1943) A theory of human motivation *Psychological Review* 50 370–396.

Reed, M. Walker, R. (eds) (2015) *A Critical Companion to Early Childhood* London: Sage

Waller, T. Davis, G. (3rd) (2014) *An Introduction to Early Childhood* London: Sage

Willan, J. Parker-Rees, R. Savage, J. (eds) (2005) *Early Childhood Studies* Exeter: Learning Matters Ltd

8 Music in the early years

John Stafford

Overview

This chapter discusses soundLINCS programmes and developmental musical projects within the sector, including private voluntary and independent settings (PVI), children's centres, childminder groups and maintained settings. Through successful funding applications and deeply rooted partnerships soundLINCS will describe how programmes were developed and adapted to suit changing circumstances within the sector. A research study conducted in partnership with Bishop Grosseteste University examined the impact of soundLINCS' early years programmes and an overview from this work will be included here.

soundLINCS is a not-for-profit community music organisation based in Lincolnshire, operating across the East Midlands. soundLINCS provides and develops high quality and innovative music-making opportunities for all ages and communities through strong partnerships.

soundLINCS's vision is simply that 'everyone has an opportunity to be empowered through music.' During its 19-year history the company has made a major contribution to the transformation of the musical landscape of Lincolnshire and the East Midlands by initiating, developing and delivering music programmes, workforce development, information, resources and research services across a wide range of genres.

> ### Reflections
>
> *Trevarthen has highlighted the importance of music for young children's language and communication. It also impacts positively on numerous other aspects of children's development.*
> *How many can you name?*

soundLINCS commenced with a part-time director in 1998 and has grown to include a staff team of 8, a Board of Trustees comprising 7 dedicated volunteers and a freelance workforce exceeding 30 musicians and artists. The company operates from a building base in Lincoln although its digital reach encompasses an international audience.

soundLINCS has been successfully developing and delivering music making programmes for Lincolnshire early years settings since 2003. A relationship with the early years sector commenced much earlier through discussions with strategic organisations to establish a Youth Music Action Zone (YMAZ) in Lincolnshire. Action Zones were an initiative from the National Foundation for Youth Music (also known as Youth Music), and 24 were established nationally. Youth Music took the view that all children and young people should have access to music opportunities, with a particular emphasis on those 'at risk' which included the importance of targeting known areas of social and economic need, providing music-making opportunities to children and young people who are socially marginalised or have educational or behavioural problems. Youth Music established three further priority areas that are particularly relevant for this chapter: early years, singing, and workforce development.

The idea of an ambitious Lincolnshire YMAZ arose in 2000 and was collaboratively developed over a period of 18 months by soundLINCS and Lincolnshire County Council (LCC). Both organisations envisaged a sustained music project of exceptional quality that would engage children and young people in a sincere music-making process. The idea, fuelled by a dedicated consortium of funders, supporters and partners, grew to be the loudest and hottest participatory music project that Lincolnshire has ever experienced. The Lincolnshire YMAZ ('sound 52') was established in August 2002 and commenced delivery of music-making projects in January 2003, including early years activities. sound52 completed in 2013 when Youth Music closed Action Zone investments and developed other funding priorities, particularly musical inclusion and work with children in challenging circumstances. Though sound52 concluded, many of its developmental projects and models of work continue to this day, including opportunities for early years music making. For more information about sound52 please visit

www.soundlincs.org/project/sound52/

soundLINCS developed relationships with many Lincolnshire early years funders and partners during the lifetime of sound52, including:

Lincolnshire County Council Early Years Support Service
Lincolnshire Early Years Development and Childcare Partnership (EYDCP)
Lincolnshire Pre-school Learning Alliance (PLA)
National Childminding Association (NCMA)
Lincolnshire Birth to Five Service
Centre for British Teaching (CfBT)

Early years non-maintained settings from the private, voluntary and independent (PVI) sector

Early years maintained settings

Every relationship was considered to be unique and consciously nurtured. It is understood that all successful projects (early years or otherwise) require partnerships of mutuality rather than a simple provider/client exchange. soundLINCS developed an expertise in early years work through its collaboration with early years funders, partners and music facilitators. A number of programmes have been developed and delivered since 2003; the following section provides a chronological overview of the these.

Reflections

What musical experiences do you provide the babies and young children you are involved with?

Have you visited other musical experiences with them, such as a toddler music group, musical show or visiting musicians?

First Notes

soundLINCS' first early years music-making programme was called First Notes. It was conceived and designed collaboratively by soundLINCS, its team of early years music facilitators and Lincolnshire PLA. Initially offered to the PVI sector, First Notes was funded as part of sound52 (Lincolnshire YMAZ) and attracted match funding from the seven city, district and borough councils of Lincolnshire, as well as Lincolnshire County Council, Lincs EYDCP, Lincs PLA and Lincs Youth Service.

First Notes' structure and content was developed by a team of eight early years music facilitators and staff from soundLINCS and Lincs PLA. The containing structure was called a residency and comprised eight weekly sessions of two hours' duration. One music facilitator was appointed to lead the residency. Each session was divided into three 40-minute blocks. The blocks provided music-making experiences and opportunities for three distinct audiences: children, practitioners and parents and carers. The intentions were that:

- the music facilitator would lead activities with the children and practitioner(s)
- the music facilitator would lead training and development activities with a group of setting practitioners. This would typically include building confidence for leading

music and singing activities; acquiring playing skills and building repertoire with tuned and untuned percussion; developing whole-group approaches for singing, playing and composition; land inking music-making activities to the Early Years Foundation Stage (EYFS)

• the music facilitator would lead activities with parents and carers to support and develop music making in the home including confidence building, singing, instrument making, using 'found' objects as instruments, simple rhythm and composition games

Each of the eight weekly sessions offered a specific core musical skill or experience that could be explored through musical games, songs and rhymes, musical instruments and composition. It was left for the music facilitator to decide how to engage children and practitioners in the specific learning core for each session. The decision-making was typically guided by the musical skills and strengths of the music facilitator and the needs and interests of the children and practitioners within any particular setting. The seven specific cores were pulse, tempo, rhythm, pitch, dynamics, exploring musical instruments and instrument-making. The eighth session included an informal sharing, to which parents and carers were invited, for children and practitioners to share what they had developed during their residency.

soundLINCS provided a First Notes instrument kit for music facilitators to use during their residency. The kit contained 54 high-quality and robust instruments that offered all children (and adults!) an exciting sound world to explore. The kit contained tuned and untuned instruments that could be struck, scraped, shaken and stirred. Identical instrument kits were provided to Lincolnshire Toy Library so that settings could loan instruments that they had become familiar with for children and families to continue their music making. Every setting that hosted a First Notes residency was given a free First Notes resource pack which is described in detail below (see p. 127).

Over time, First Notes developed to include an offer for maintained settings whilst also continuing in the PVI sector. The structure was reduced to six weekly sessions to reflect the adoption of the six-term timetable in Lincolnshire. The structure was further adapted to ensure a more flexible offer to settings. This included, for example, reducing session durations to one hour for settings that could not easily accommodate parent/carer sessions or dedicated practitioner groups. This adaption also recognised that many settings were receiving repeat residencies.

Work with practitioners always incorporated an element of mentoring and, as First Notes returned to settings for a second or third time, this became the dominant form of training and development. Creating a bespoke programme of support for early years settings was developed from First Notes experiences and a new programme called Root Notes became available. Root Notes is described in detail below.

soundLINCS made direct contact with every maintained and PVI setting in Lincolnshire commencing in 2003. This was primarily achieved through regular telephone contact and frequent mailouts of promotional materials and booking forms.

1,696 First Notes residencies have been completed, resulting in 12,160 sessions being delivered. 31,419 children have participated together with 3,540 parents/carers and 5,218 practitioners.

Reflections

Which aspects of music does the child or children you work with enjoy most?
Which instruments, either bought or made, do they enjoy playing?

Music Sounds Inclusive

Music Sounds Inclusive, as part of sound52, was an innovative music project for the 0–5 age group. It was piloted in 2005–6 in a selection of venues in Lincolnshire, and was subsequently successfully rolled out across the county. Music Sounds Inclusive was dedicated to developing music-making opportunities for childminders so they could open up access to participatory music-making for the children in their care.

The programme was developed in partnership with the National Childminding Association (NCMA) and combined accredited training for childminders as part of the NCMA Gold Star Awards. It also provided the pre-school children in their care opportunities to explore participatory music-making within a creative and socially inclusive environment.

The project was set up in a selection of community-based venues around the county for up to 12 childminders and their early years children to attend. The venues were typically community centres, children's centres and village halls. Two early years music facilitators worked together to lead the sessions and were equipped with instrument kits designed to meet specific early years needs. The groups (childminders and children) participated in two structured daytime music workshops of one hour's duration, usually a week apart. These were separated by an evening training session of two hours' duration solely for the childminders, in which fundamental musical concepts such as rhythm, pulse, dynamics and pitch were explored alongside the wider social and educational benefits of creative music-making within a group environment.

Music Sounds Inclusive provided a small set of instruments for each participating childminder and included the recording and distribution of a music CD featuring songs written and sung by the childminders.

Music Sounds Inclusive was further developed in partnership with Lincolnshire Birth to Five service and guided by the theme 'making music with a varied age group.' The structure was identical to the original design and offered two daytime group sessions of two hours' duration with children and one evening training session of two hours' duration for child minders. The daytime sessions focused on music-making activities for 0–5's and the evening session explored ideas for holidays when the children in the childminder's care might cover a much broader age range.

In total 33 residencies have been completed, resulting in 99 sessions being delivered. Some 495 children, 20 parents/carers and 396 childminders have participated.

Early Ears

Early Ears was originally developed in 2009 for children's centres, in partnership with Lincolnshire County Council (and in conjunction with the Every Child Matters initiative) and the Centre for British Teaching (CfBT). CfBT, at that time, were providing the School Improvement Service for Lincolnshire together with core services for children's centres through, for example, early years practitioners. Early Ears was initially programmed for Phase 1 and 2 children's centres. Phase 1 centres were developed to serve families living in the 20 per cent of wards that were most disadvantaged. Phase 2 centres were developed to ensure all of the most disadvantaged families (i.e. those in the 30 per cent of areas at greatest disadvantage) would have access to children's centre services. Early Ears also became available for post-Phase 2 children's centres over time.

soundLINCS designed the music programme for children aged 0–5 years and their parents/carers, offering opportunities for parents with one or more children the chance to participate in music-making together.

The core offer provided each children's centre with 24 two-hour sessions which were divided into four blocks of six. Each block was scheduled for the same day and time each week. Additionally, each centre was offered three full days that were flexibly designed and arranged to suit each centre's specific needs, for example by providing music activities for family fun days and during school holiday periods. Additional projects at individual centres, such as music technology sessions for older children during school holiday times, ran on a bespoke basis.

Early Ears was delivered by an experienced soundLINCS early years music facilitator and each children's centre was provided with a comprehensive kit of musical instruments, funded by Lincolnshire County Council.

The soundLINCS music facilitator was a mentor, trainer and supporter who provided early years practitioners with ideas, information and guidance on providing fun and accessible music activities to groups of young children and their parents/carers. Each residency delivered bespoke Early Ears provision to meet the needs of its users and community, with all music-making activities related to the EYFS. soundLINCS music facilitators were engaged on a termly basis to meet each children's centre's individual requirements. For example, some centres utilised Early Ears provision for mother and baby sessions, whilst others opted to use provision for staff training, for carers of learning-disabled children or to encourage music-making amongst groups for whom English was not their first language.

The priority aims of the programme were:

- To enable practitioners to develop new skills to effectively deliver high quality musical experiences to children and young people they support.

- For practitioners and parents/carers to gain confidence to use music to engage and develop children and young people's learning opportunities.

- For practitioners to receive appropriate support and training so they could sustain the key elements of the project independently.

- To enable children to access and participate in high-quality, creative music activities, and progress at a differentiated and appropriate level of development.

- To enable practitioners to use creative musical activities alongside other forms of communication in order to help children voice their thoughts, ideas and feelings.

Early Ears+

An extension to the original Early Ears programme, Early Ears+ enabled children's centres to explore new approaches and methodologies to develop the skills and confidence of early years children.

Early Ears music activities were ideal for family fun and group interaction, whilst developing motor, sensory and linguistic skills together with stretching the children's capacity for learning. Early Ears+ used this platform to deliver lively, hands-on sessions which included music and movement, music and storytelling and music and theatre.

Early Ears is a very flexible model that has been adapted to reflect the changing needs of the children's centre sector. In 2012–13, for example, ten residencies were provided to children's centres in partnership with the Lincolnshire Birth to Five Service as a workforce development programme for practitioners working with early years children at elevated risk. In 2014–16, for example, 14 residencies were provided to children's centres in partnership with CfBT as a workforce development programme for children's centre practitioners. Both these initiatives combined aspects of Early Ears and Root Notes (see p. 124) to initiate a gradual shifting for group planning and leadership from soundLINCS music facilitators to children's centre practitioners.

Early Ears developed a resource pack designed to support parents/carers to initiate and develop music-making within the home. Details of the resource pack are included below.

Early Ears in its many guises has completed 72 residencies, resulting in 648 sessions being delivered. In total 1,313 children, 31 parents/carers and 284 practitioners have participated.

My Musical Day

My Musical Day commenced in 2012 and completed in 2013. It was a sound52 programme developed by soundLINCS and the Birth to Five service. It was developed alongside the UK government's initiative 'Every Child a Talker,' with the aim of engaging children in music-making to stimulate and encourage verbal communication with their parents, carers, practitioners and peers. It was predominantly hosted in children's centres and early years PVI settings. It engaged early years children, parents/carers and early years and children's centre Practitioners.

The project offered simple techniques which could be continued in the home or setting environment, and was fast-paced and engaging for the children and accompanying adults.

The programme was aimed at children of 0–5 years and was particularly advantageous to those at elevated risk, specifically those with special education needs (SEN), English as an additional language (EAL) and those at social and economic disadvantage. The programme was offered to communities identified as having an elevated risk.

My Musical Day was structured around a menu of topics from which each setting could select. Each topic took around 45 minutes to complete and included:

- Song bank
- Family bonding
- Bettering bedtimes
- Start your day with a song
- Instrument making
- Communicating emotions

To date 10 residencies have been completed, resulting in 46 sessions being delivered. A total of 138 children, 68 parents/carers and 36 practitioners have participated.

Root Notes

Root Notes was developed in 2011 in partnership with Lincolnshire Birth to Five Service. It draws on learning from previous early years programmes, particularly First Notes and Early Ears. Both of these programmes have a core offer of workforce development for early years practitioners and Root Notes is a logical and imaginative response to the learning gained from them.

The containing structure for Root Notes is a residency. Each residency comprises nine one-hour sessions arranged over 18 weeks. The residency has an alternating pattern in which the soundLINCS early years music facilitator delivers the odd numbered sessions and the setting practitioner delivers the even numbered sessions. The music facilitator's role is that of trainer, mentor and advisor to the practitioner/s, manager and the setting. The facilitator's aim is to shift the primary responsibility for planning and delivering sessions away from themselves and towards the practitioner over the 18-week programme. They achieve this by enabling practitioners to develop confidence, skills, knowledge and experience to independently lead music activities with early years children. The ultimate goal is to increase and sustain high-quality music activities for early years children with the attendant benefits to their personal, social and emotional development (PSED), communication and creativity.

Root Notes is supported by a Root Notes resource pack containing two key resources:

- A diary-style journal for practitioners to log achievements made, reflections for development and ideas to develop music-making sessions and activities. Practitioners are encouraged to use ideas and suggestions provided by the soundLINCS music facilitator and to record their own thoughts and suggestions for improvements to their music delivery. The journal has been designed to incorporate written and/or photographic evidence.
- A Root Notes tree poster presented to the setting at the beginning of their residency and used to display the achievements and progress made.

The communication between the music facilitator and the setting manager and practitioner is absolutely key to the success of the residency. It is vital that the manager and practitioner 'own' the Root Notes process and feel completely engaged in it. To enable this relationship, the music facilitator will ensure that they spend time with the practitioner before and after each facilitator-led session, to reflect on successes and challenges and to identify viable action plans for the remaining sessions. The Root Notes diary is an important document for this process. It contains an outcomes table that the manager and practitioner will select from to establish a number of goals that will be worked towards during the residency. The outcomes reflect many aspects of the EYFS and the principles of inclusive practice. A minimum of 9 outcomes are selected from a list of 18.

Practitioner outcomes

Mandatory outcome:

- At least one practitioner has increased confidence in leading early years songs, and leading regular vocal or instrumental activities (possibly through the First Notes resource pack).

Please choose at least two outcomes from this list:

- To develop own musical activities in the setting, possibly by extending activities from the First Notes resource pack.
- Develop skills in early years composition by using graphic scores, colour coding systems and poem writing.
- Gain awareness of existing national music initiatives and use these resources.
- For at least one practitioner to attend a creative CPD training day and share the new knowledge with colleagues.
- Practitioner creates own outcome.

Cross-curricular outcomes

Please choose at least two outcomes from this list:

- Be able to adapt musical activities to be inclusive of children with English as a second language and also children with disabilities.
- Create a song bank in your setting of songs that can adapted to reflect moods, feeling or emotions. This song bank should also be used as a two-way listening and communication tool.
- Refurbish or create an indoor and outdoor environment for making music; in addition develop a musical sensory area or activities.
- Create a musical activity or game that includes physical movement and that helps children learn a skill in another curriculum area (e.g. the alphabet, counting, days of the week).

Reflections

What skills are needed to work with babies and young children when accessing musical activities?
Which skills are essential and which are desirable?

Setting outcomes

Please choose at least three outcomes from this list:

- Spring-clean resources.

- The setting creates a sensory musical area (soundLINCS can provide ideas and guidelines for this).
- Develop a repertoire of music activities suitable for all age groups in the setting. Provide opportunities to integrate the 0–2s with the 3–5s in some music activities.
- Develop a repertoire for indoor and outdoor music activities that can be easily accessed by the children during all play times.
- Commit to provide at least one musical experience each day.

Please choose at least one outcome from this list:

- Devise and deliver a medium-term music celebration event.
- Design, create and use a selection of early years instruments.
- Compose an anthem/song and perform it for the setting.

Music facilitators tailored each residency to reflect the needs of the practitioner within the setting. Some practitioners, for example, preferred the music facilitator to engage children during the facilitator-led sessions, whilst others preferred those sessions to be spent focused on them. In most cases, a balance between these two positions was provided.

Root Notes settings were selected by the Birth to Five service for support, reward, to focus attention on current agendas (such as provision for two-year-olds) or to engage newly qualified early years professionals.

In total 72 residencies were completed, resulting in 648 sessions being delivered. To date 1,313 children and 284 practitioners have participated.

First Notes resource pack

The First Notes resource pack was originally developed, printed and published in 2004. It was revised, redesigned, reprinted and republished in a second edition in 2008, in response to the new Early Years Foundation Stage (EYFS), which became effective from September 2008. A further revised third edition was produced in 2016 and developed in digital form as a mobile app for both iOS and Android platforms. It incorporates the most recent changes to the EYFS, including the development of prime and specific areas of learning and development, which are shown as intrinsically linked to the characteristics for effective learning.

Every early years setting in Lincolnshire has received a free copy of the printed First Notes resource pack. The development of the mobile app enables settings to stay up to date with the latest version and download as many instances as they require.

The idea of a First Notes resource pack was originally conceived in 2001 by soundLINCS and its Lincolnshire partners in the context of a funding application to establish sound52, the Lincolnshire Youth Music Action Zone. The partners in developing the original pack were soundLINCS, Lincolnshire EYDCP, Lincolnshire PLA, Lincolnshire County Council Curriculum Advisors and First Notes music facilitators. The intention behind the First Note Resource Pack was to develop a flexible package of activities that can be used in two distinct ways:

- Practitioners could follow a musical path through the pack and select activities that were linked either by category (pulse, tempo, pitch etc.) or by theme (shared instrument set, turn taking, use of the spoken word etc.).
- Practitioners could follow a curriculum path through the pack and select activities that were linked by the EYFS.

The updating of the First Notes Resource Pack 2nd Edition was commissioned by Lincolnshire Birth to Five Service (a service managed by CfBT on behalf of Lincolnshire County Council), who had significant input into the new structure along with soundLINCS and First Notes music facilitators.

The First Notes Mobile App is an exciting new music resource for use in early years settings or by parents and carers at home – especially those without any previous experience of music. It features exercises and activities designed to suit all ability levels, to help with a child's development in and outside of music. The app links directly with the areas of learning and development covered by the EYFS, allowing practitioners in early years settings to complete EYFS Profiles and build their own schemes of work. For parents and carers, the app provides a range of fun and creative ways to bring music into the home by engaging young children in activities tailored to their continued development.

The app features over 60 unique activities split into categories, from name games and warm-ups through to instrument-making tutorials that demonstrate how to create instruments to use with the app. The category menus are easy to find and can be selected by simply swiping a finger. Having the right category, all of the activities are listed ready to be used.

The app has been designed to enable progressive learning and development in music to meet every child's needs. The pages are split into sections that explain the activity and where to start. Eventually, the **When child is ready, move on** sections enable new challenges and enhance skills, keeping the activities fun and dynamic for all ages between birth and five years old. This means that there are over 120 creative exercises for use with all children in the EY age range.

Many of the pages include Music Tracks, playable at the touch of a button, which demonstrate and accompany the songs found in an activity. Lyrics and actions for each song on the pages and the instrumental version of each track provides a reassuring backing to sing along to. A full list of all 45 tracks can be accessed through the Quick Menu for fast and easy selection.

As well as helping with progression, each activity on the App contains an **Inclusivity** section providing useful suggestions to promote inclusivity when carrying out any exercise. Adapting the activity for use with Hearing-Impaired and those with reduced mobility makes the App suitable for use with everyone.

Links for free downloading of The First Notes Mobile App can found on the soundLINCS website www.soundlincs.org/2016/06/first-notes-app-share-special/

Early Ears resource pack

The Early Ears resource pack was developed, printed and distributed in 2010 in partnership with Lincolnshire Birth to Five Service. It was developed by soundLINCS especially for use at home by parents/carers of EY children. It draws upon professional experiences gathered over a decade of music-making with young children. Similar to the First Notes resource pack, it is especially suitable those without any previous experience of music.

The pack contains ten A5 double-sided laminate cards in a durable wallet. There are eight activity cards in the pack, including ideas for songs, expressive vocal sounds, movement, instrument-making, simple percussion games and composition. Each activity is described with three progressive musical steps, and suggestions for resources and adaptions for making each activity accessible for all. Each activity card also includes fun facts that widen the context of music activities by describing the wider benefits of participating in playing and singing.

Early years resource packs have been given freely to parents, carers and practitioners involved in children's centre programmes.

soundBEGINNINGS

soundLINCS obtained funding from Youth Music to undertake an early years research study based on the company's programmes (as described above) for the period 2003–2013. The study, titled 'soundBEGINNINGS: ten years of early years development,' was conducted with Professor Chris Atkin and Dr Pat Beckley from Bishop Grosseteste University. Dr Beckley undertook the role of lead researcher.

The study aimed to evaluate and harness the perception of impact, disseminate and share the experience of 10 years of music education development within the early years sector in Lincolnshire. A secondary objective was to produce a series of good practice case studies based on the research across a range of early years settings.

Five members of soundLINCS staff formed the team that coordinated the study and undertook visits to early years settings to conduct research interviews with practitioners. The team attended a research development day with Professor Atkin and Dr Beckley before commencing any research activities.

The research study identified 14 settings, selected to represent a diverse range of provision types (large, small, maintained, PVI, children's centres), localities (urban, rural, county-wide) and programmes (First Notes, Early Ears, Root Notes). A number of settings (particularly maintained settings) declined to participate in the study, citing staff shortages or lack of staff capacity for interviews: the research team identified suitable replacement settings. Face-to-face interviews were conducted with 12 practitioners at a representative range of early years settings. Interviews were based on a set of questions agreed with Dr Beckley. They gathered information about typical music activities facilitated by the setting, and considered availability of CPD for practitioners, recollection of soundLINCS visits to the setting and summary of any perceived impact, knowledge and use of soundLINCS resource packs.

A second development day for the research team was facilitated by Professor Atkin and Dr Beckley when the 12 interviews were completed. The purpose of the day was to review and discuss the information gathered from the interviews and agree a structure for presenting the findings of the study. The agreed structure was to collect the study findings under five headings; the section below highlights key findings.

The role of the child

The role of the child within an early years setting is obviously crucial, however the role of the child when looking at the organisation of music provision within a setting is not immediately obvious. One of the first threshold concepts we will look at is that of *organisation*. One of the basic assumptions about a music workshop is that it is noisy, chaotic and hard work. Children love noise and are happy to experiment with all instruments; at first they have no immediate distinction between what is a good sound and what is discordant. Through our research we have discovered that a good music session is one where the communication is simple and practical. To communicate the boundaries of the session before dishing out the instruments is a good way to make sure you are heard. Teaching the basic practices of start/stop, louder/quieter – preferably with some sort of visual signal – can be a great way to keep the music session under your control. With a greater variety of interactive activities, including props baskets and song bags, the children can choose what happens next.

Engaging the children in this way gives them more ownership of the session – in other words, it enables them to be in the session. Creatively developing the sessions so that they become multi-arts activities allows children to experience music in a variety of ways. Increasing the amount of movement in the session keeps the children engaged and has developmental benefits. Other art forms can also have a good result; crafting your own instruments, outdoor music sessions. Music is well known for overcoming language barriers and has the advantage of being very practical, which can also help with disengaged children. Music sessions enable the practitioners to treat all the children as unique and individual. Recognising that all children have the capacity to be both creative and musical is essential when leading an activity: even the most introverted child will be able to join in at a level that is comfortable to them. Even listening is still taking part. Developing good relationships with the facilitators or practitioners allows the children to build up the confidence to speak up and lead activities; repeated use of the musical resources gives them confidence to approach the musical instrument stations and play with them, coming up with song ideas, lyrics and new tunes. It even allows them to get creative and make their own instruments.

The role of the practitioner, then, includes impact as a key champion disseminating practice and supporting delivery, as well as enhancing positive relationships with children and developing new skills.

soundLINCS identified the following key aspects of a practitioner's role when leading music sessions:

- Key champions – one who does
- Supporting delivery
- Interactions with children – positive relationship
- Development of new skills

When practitioners were able to engage with the children at their individual development levels this had a huge impact on the quality of the session. An awareness of early childhood development was essential.

An important factor considered was the creative environment, including its impact on resources used, measures to support an enabling environment, active learning and creative approaches.

At a large forest school nursery the children were allowed to make their own choices about the types of activities they do. Based within the grounds of a working farm, the nursery allows children regularly to go out on forest school expeditions and adventures. As well as having a selection of traditional instruments, they also made their own instruments from sticks and natural materials outside, and once this skill had been shown to a child by a practitioner, or passed on to them by a peer, they were in a position to be able to access and play musically at their own will.

The children in another setting were encouraged to explore sounds all around them, and were never told that the way they choose to play an instrument was 'wrong.' If a child put toy cars inside an inverted drum to hear what noise it made the practitioners praised the way in which the child was exploring.

Many of the settings visited demonstrated musical play with resources that would not necessarily be considered to be musical. Some offered music in both a formal and an ad-hoc way. It was up to the children in some cases to initiate music making. Settings varied in the routines used for musical inputs. Some had daily defined times for music while others incorporated musical interludes throughout the day as the activities arose.

Many nurseries displayed an innovative use of resources to offer musical opportunities to the children. For example, at one nursery the manager liked to surprise the children, so often picked up instruments from the local charity shop and introduced them to the room – without saying anything... She just liked to see the children go and explore a new instrument for themselves without being told in the first place what its purpose was or how it was used. She watched how the children shared their findings with each other.

The study considered also the external environment, including the programmes' impact on community involvement, Ofsted reports and the EYFS framework.

As noted, the research involved several different types of settings, including children's centres, forest schools, independent nurseries, pre-schools feeding into schools on the same site and playgroups.

Parents wanted to experience a music programme that offered them activities that they could expand upon and use at home with their children. The forest school environment lent itself well to musical development: the various qualities of wood can be used to demonstrate different timbres, while the surrounding natural environment can help young explorers to discover a range of tonalities all from readily available materials.

In the pre-school activities included a Christmas presentation that the children perform along with the main school, partaking in assemblies. Music is a large part of this presentation. The pre-school also provided a book for each of the children with their favourite songs in it for them to take with them into the Reception class.

Lastly the study considered soundLINCS resources, including the impact of resource packs, CPD and workforce development activities, and the influence of soundLINCS early years music facilitators.

soundLINCS has used resource packs to facilitate musical activities, particularly where practitioners lack confidence in this crucial area of learning and development. Activities and resources have been used to encourage and enhance children's awareness, enjoyment and knowledge of sounds and music around them.

At one with nature

Pat Beckley and Karin Moen

Overview

The chapter describes the doctoral research undertaken by Pat Beckley, leading visits for English trainee teachers and staff to Norwegian *barnehages* and *skoles* (which accommodate nursery-aged children and those in school respectively) in the Hedmark region, and exploring their reflections on their experiences there. Insights into the philosophy behind the culture of being 'at one with nature' were considered. These were shared with colleagues, particularly Karin Moen, who developed the visitors' understanding of the philosophy. This was considered further and reflected upon, as is discussed in the chapter. Finally, the chapter explores how the philosophy is used in the approach to learning in the early years, both in Norway and England.

Visits to Norwegian early years settings

The initial insights into a different philosophy began when a group of Norwegian early years teachers visited England and gave a well-received presentation about their work and how it was underpinned by the philosophy of being 'at one with nature.' As experienced English early years teachers mainly used to allowing their young children short bursts of 10–15 minutes' fresh air outdoors with a 'run-around,' it came as a surprise to hear of settings where children could explore their surroundings and activities with learning taking place largely outdoors. This presentation engrossed practitioners and a group of four visited the area to observe what was going on and how it was achieved! The visit provided insights into a different culture. Firstly, the weather needed careful consideration. Cars driving and people walking across the frozen lakes took a while to comprehend. A pleasant walk in the sunshine, followed by three hours spent attempting to return to the hotel in the changed freezing weather, with a slight detour as we became lost in snow-filled poor visibility, quickly helped us to respect the power and force of nature and our surroundings. A doctoral study followed, with wonderment at the similar early years policies but different approaches to their implementation in the two countries. Further discussion and presentations followed and an interest in observing the philosophy from trainee teachers and university colleagues led to annual visits to Norwegian settings.

The visits fostered similar responses from the students each year. Rising early to catch the cheapest flights, a long train journey and finally our destination at a 'Pensjonat' boarding house, meant the students were tired by the time night fell. Comments such a 'It's just like England' were common, as the visitors spotted the global food outlet logo in the nearby town centre. During the subsequent week visits to the barnhages and skoles followed. As the visitors learned more about the settings they visited and the learning approaches used, they reflected on aspects they had seen. The open environment of the settings astonished them, followed by the attitude to taking risks and accessing activities. 'Was that really a child climbing the tree outside the school?' 'Was that child asleep at the top of the tree?' 'Why does the three-year-old have a hammer?' 'The five-year-old is chopping down a tree with an axe, helped by an adult holding the tree.' 'Those children are making shelters in the snow.' 'This group of four-year-olds are helping the adult to make a fire!' These activities seem to have been unheard of and caused surprise, sometimes alarm, at the competence and lack of fear of the youngest children.

When visiting the barnhages children played happily in the snow, devising pathways with their cars, trucks and snowclearers, climbing trees and bushes, skating, skiing or sliding on ice, role playing with the natural artefacts outdoors such as branches for kitchens and stoves, looking for signs of animal life or building dens and snow shelters. These activities were observed by the adults present, who interacted with the children to develop the child's ideas, experiences and concepts of the world around them. Areas of the curriculum such as physical development, mathematics, language and communicating were interwoven as part of a progressive, personalised way of developing and enhancing knowledge and understandings through activities in context that were meaningful to each child. The activities were underpinned by the notion of working together as a social community, supporting each other and developing the self to promote the work of all in the group.

The English students' initial observation that the small town visited seemed very much like an English one gave way to a gradual realisation that the philosophy providing the foundations for the thinking and approach was different to that experienced in England. There followed reflections about why it could be different. Was it the weather causing a need to be aware and be prepared for the cold conditions of the long winter? Was it the population numbers, with 5 million in Norway compared to 62 million in England, giving a sense of space, openness and quiet? It had been noted on the train that there were carriages designated 'Stille' and intended to be silent, with passages on board them looking at the scenery beyond the window or silently reading or knitting. Could the difference be the personality of the inhabitants, who enjoyed the stillness and peace of their surroundings?

Collaboration for philosophical reflections

Karin arranged a mid-week discussion between the English students and colleagues, as well as Norwegian professors from the local university, who described the rationale behind the approaches. This rationale included a love for the outdoors and national legislation that meant Norwegians were able to roam through the countryside as they wished, taking care of their environment. It also highlighted an emphasis on oneness with nature, enjoying it but being part of it – nature was a force in itself to be reckoned with and respected. Finally, there was a dog-sleigh ride, taking participants through the frozen countryside in silence, with only the sounds of the swish of the rails in the snow and the breath of the dogs. This must be truly to be at one with nature, when there is a sense that the body reverts to its molecular structure and becomes part of the atmosphere.

Case study

On a dog-sleigh ride in Norway there was an intense, quiet peacefulness, where oneness with nature comprised interaction: nature became part of oneself, or the self melted into the surrounding natural environment. The brain processes the harmony of being at one with nature and seems to gain a new independence of thinking.

In Norway, from an early age, children are encouraged to explore the outdoors. They access a barnehage for childcare, a house where they can grow. Outdoor provision forms an integral aspect of the learning, with babies and toddlers having time to sleep outdoors if they are tired and explorations centred around the nature space. Children are able to gain an awareness of their environment and how to appreciate it and be safe in it.

Reflections

Do you use an outdoor environment for exploration and learning in your setting?
What does it consist of?
What would you like to include to enable the enhancement of the provision?

Table 9.1 Education stages in Norway

Age	Legal status	Provision type
1–5 years	Non-compulsory entitlement	Early childhood education (private and public)
6–15 years	Compulsory education	Grunnskole (mostly public), consisting of: 1–7th grade: Barnetrinnet, primary school 8–10th grade: Ungdomstrinnet, lower secondary school
16–19 years	Non-compulsory entitlement	11–13th grade: Videregående – upper secondary (mostly public)
19 years +	Non-compulsory, no automatic entitlement	University

The Norwegian education system

Early childhood education (or *barnehage*: 'barn' means 'child' and 'hage' means 'garden') in Norway is part of the education system, and is operated under the Ministry of Education. Children are not obliged to attend early childhood education, but they are entitled to do so from when they are a year old. In Norway children start school in August the year they turn six. This means that some children are 6 ½ when they start school and some are only 5 ½. Schooling is compulsory, with 10 years of education, and everyone is entitled to three years at upper secondary (see Table 9.1).

In Norway, early childhood education can be either private or public; either type of provision follows the same laws and guidelines and has the same framework plan (curriculum). Schools are mostly public. In early childhood education, parents pay a monthly fee; all schools are however free.

Norwegian culture

Norway is a country where the people live close to nature. At the beginning of the 20th century, Norway was one of the poorest countries in Europe. Then came the discovery of oil in the 1960s: things changed, but Norway remains a very equal society, without for instance a nobility. For long periods of history people lived in rather small houses and had many children, meaning that the space available for activities was limited. To survive under these conditions, children had to stay outdoor to complete their activities, as well as helping their mothers and fathers with work related to the household. Even adults spent a lot of time outdoors: further back in history this time would have been spent gathering provisions to survive – fishing, hunting, picking berries, or growing their own vegetable and crops. Later time outdoors came to include enjoying activities more for pleasure, like skiing, skating, walking, climbing and swimming, though gathering food from nature also remained important.

Most Norwegians spend time surrounded by nature every week; walking in summer, skiing in winter. Many have their own cottage by the sea or in the mountains where they carry out different activities during all seasons. Such cottages used to be very small, simple and standard, but now many people use them more like a second home with all facilities.

Norwegian early childhood education

When early childhood education was first introduced from the middle of the 19th century, good health was an important issue. Many of the children in early childhood education settings came from poor homes, therefore fresh air and physical activities were important for good health.

Early childhood education was until the 1970s the province of the few. From then onwards, though, it became more common, as increasing numbers of women entered full-time work. Today about 90 per cent of all children in Norway attend early childhood education from about one year of age until six. As an extension of the pervasiveness of outdoor activity in ordinary life, early childhood education in Norway too embraced a tradition of outdoor activity, not only outdoor play.

Einarsdottir and Wagner (2006, p. 4) describe the Norwegian barnehage thus: "Child and family policies are based on Nordic ideology and traditions, emphasizing democracy, equality, freedom and emancipation, solidarity through cooperation and compromise, and general concept of the 'good childhood'". This child-centeredness is an important part of the adults' approach to the children and their activity. This is, as Einarsdottir and Wagner say, an essential value in a democratic upbringing. The framework says:

> The Kindergartens shall meet the children with trust and respect, and acknowledge the intrinsic value of childhood. They shall contribute to well-being and joy in play and learning, and shall be a challenging and safe place for community life and friendship. The Kindergarten shall promote democracy and equality and counteract all forms of discrimination.
>
> (Ministry for Education and Research, 2011, p. 7)

This is one of the main reasons why the children's own activities, initiative and voice are essential in daily work. The teacher is the guide in an upbringing directed towards democratic thinking.

Curriculum for early childhood education

Norwegian early childhood settings have their own framework describing learning objectives, subject areas and working methods. Children's own activities and participation are important elements in education and development aimed at a democratic understanding and value base. The elements are central to all activities in the early childhood education, both inside and outside.

The framework for Norwegian early childhood education says:

> Outdoor exploration and experiences can encourage environmental awareness and a desire in children to protect our natural resources, preserve biodiversity and contribute to sustainable development. Early childhood education shall enable the children to appreciate nature and have outdoor experiences that teach them to move around and spend time in the outdoors during the different seasons.
>
> Early childhood education shall enable the children to enjoy a variety of outdoor experiences and discover nature as an arena for play and learning. Early childhood education shall stimulate the children to remain curious about natural phenomena, feel connected to nature and gain experience of using technology and tools.
>
> (Ministry of Education and Research, 2014)

So, from the beginnings of early childhood education in the 19th century up until today, outdoor activity has been more than just good for the children's health: it stimulates various parts of children's development and is essential in a democratic upbringing.

Learning by playing

Norwegian early childhood education has always had a large focus on play and on learning through play. Free play has always occupied an important role. This understanding has its roots in the thinking of Froebel, and later that of Piaget, Vygotsky and Leontiev. These theorists have great significance for our knowledge of the importance that play has for the child's development and learning. More recently there has also been a focus on the meaning of the teacher's role in relation to play. In Piaget's thinking about play, the pedagogue was primarily a facilitator. For Vygotsky, Leontiev and other more modern research, the pedagogue is seen more as an active participant: sometimes with their own role in roleplaying, other times more on the sidelines as an active observer, other times still as an adult who provides input and reflection and reflects amazement together with the children. The learning potential is located in the interplay between doing (playing), amazement and reflection, both during the play and afterwards. Talking about the activity after it is complete can enhance learning by putting words to what you have done and what you have learned from it: language is an important part in the learning process. This means that you need to have teachers who are close to the children's play to be able to recognise what is happening in that play.

The importance of play and activity as central to children's learning is also reflected in the understanding of what is happening outdoors. In the barnehage, formal lessons are rare, becoming slightly more common for five-year-olds in their last year at the barnehage before they start school. In many schools too though play and outdoor activities remain common, especially during primary school.

Outdoor time in early childhood education has long been seen as simply a natural part of a day's nursery activity. Free play has long dominated, with adults participating to a lesser extent (as was also the case in fact indoors). Eventually the teachers developed increasing understanding that outdoor activities could be used more consciously and educationally. Teachers thus developed a greater appreciation for outdoor activities' huge learning potential in themselves, in line with recent research.

Learning through outdoor activities

Outdoor activity is, as we have seen, an important part of all early childhood education in Norway. The children are outdoors for a part of the day all year through, though on days when the temperature is below -20 degrees Celsius the youngest children may stay indoors. Outdoor activity can consist of play, physical activity or more organised activities like studying flowers, animals or insects, or cutting trees, making watermills and so on.

Since most early childhood education settings are located near to natural areas, there are different types of early childhood education that have a special focus on outdoor activities. In Norway such settings are called farm early childhood education, nature early childhood education, outdoor early childhood education and so on. Some such early childhood education settings have no permanent building at all, and may sometimes instead have a tent or *lavvo*, a structure somewhat similar to a tipi. The children play outdoors and eat outdoors; the youngest sleep outdoors and have their nappies changed outdoors. Children who go to such settings usually have parents who themselves are particularly interested in outdoor activities.

The teacher's role

Norwegian early childhood education has a tradition combining three interconnected themes: play, learning and care (Ministry of Education and Research, 2014). These themes are bonded. This means fundamentally that learning is primarily focused on children's natural activity, not on more formal activities. When English students visited Norwegian early childhood education provision they often asked: when will the teachers do teaching? It was difficult to understand the teacher's role when there was hardly any formal teaching.

An example of learning by outdoor activity is as follows:

Case study

The teacher is together with five children at their outdoor space in the forest. They are making a fire and then afterwards make lunch. The teacher and the children together find logs and equipment for lighting the fire. They need paper, wood shavings and matches. The teacher is explaining, but letting the children try. They learn that the logs have to be dry; that they can't make a fire with the log alone; they learn how to maintain the fire.

Then it is time to make lunch, baking bread on the fire and frying sausages. The children learn how to make the dough and how to bake it on the fire. They learn measurement and feel the consistency of the dough. The dialogue between the teacher and the children can cover a range of subjects: how do we make sausage? What does it contain? Where does the meat come from? Is it right to eat meat? How do we tidy up after having made a fire? And so on.

The dialogue can be related to current themes or be more free-ranging, drawing on the children's experimentations. The dialogue can also include topics related to the group's co-operation, or more relational questions. The teacher is an active part in this, but always lets the children try for themselves and explain their own experiences. The teacher is guiding, asking questions, explaining new words and emphasising what they have learned. The children's own voice and experiences are an important part of this learning sequence. Being part of the whole process, they will learn how things are connected, how to cooperate, how to compromise and how to solve conflicts. All this is part of a democratic upbringing.

The bachelor degree in early childhood education

In Norway you need a bachelor degree to work as a teacher in a barnehage. The degree is based on 13 years of primary, lower and upper secondary education, followed by three years of degree-level study at a university. The leader of every barnehage has a BA degree. The children are mostly organised in groups of about 10–20, depending on their age; every group has one or two degree-qualified teachers and one or two assistants with

Table 9.2 Overview of the Programme

Year 1: autumn	Year 1: spring	Year 2: autumn	Year 2: spring	Year 3: autumn	Year 3: spring
Children's play, development, learning etc.	Society, ethics, religion etc.	Art, culture and creativity		Specialisation	Management, cooperation, development etc.
	Nature, health, physical activities etc.	Language, text, mathematics etc.	Children's play, development, learning etc.		Bachelor thesis
3 weeks' practice	4 weeks' practice	4 weeks' practice	4 weeks' practice	2 weeks' practice	3 weeks' practice

education to college level. There might also be teachers trained specifically in caring for children with special needs.

The bachelor education programme is based on the official framework (Ministry of Education, 2017).

The education framework was reorganised in 2013 and is now based on knowledge areas rather than academic subjects. Students must show learning outcomes in areas of knowledge, skills and general competence. The model is illustrated in Table 9.2.

In all knowledge areas children's play and activity are central themes; they constitute the main part of the knowledge area called nature, health and physical activities.

The bachelor degree required by teachers centres on what is called in Norway the students' *danning*. *Danning* means formation, and consists of the skills and values that trainee teachers will cultivate at the university, with their fellow students and the teachers, when they conduct teaching practice placements and in their academic work. *Danning* is strongly connected to democratic values, and students are also prepared to develop the children's *danning*. Outdoor activities are one of the arenas in which this cultivation will happen.

Implementing philosophy into practice

When the English students and colleagues returned from Norway to the UK they shared their experiences with others at the university. They also became teachers, and therefore initiated programmes of outdoor activity to suit the school where they were employed. This could entail the acquisition of a designated woodland area where the children could explore natural surroundings. Planned tasks could be implemented to put learning into context, for example phonics lessons using the environment as a way to find words beginning with a certain sound. The facilities have been used throughout the year and provide an area for exploration in all weathers and seasons, such as looking for minibeasts in summer or introducing a social circle-time gathering with biscuits and hot chocolate in winter. Many learning styles are catered for and some children find the impetus of outdoor learning can provide a means to access other areas of the curriculum. It also provides a calm environment for some children who have behaviour challenges. The freedom and openness of the outdoors can provide some children with an atmosphere that lets them respond to and enjoy their learning.

Philosophy of oneness with nature

There are many possible reasons why Norwegian culture is seemingly underpinned by a love of nature; the dramatic scenery and small population promote a respect for the outdoors and natural environment it embraces. The culture is often referred to as *friluftsliv*, or 'free air life,' a term first published in Henrik Ibsen's 1859 poem 'On the Heights,' which included his reflections in an isolated, simply furnished country cottage where he could consider his thoughts. McLendon (2014) states 'The Norwegian word, coined in 1859, has come to embody Norway's cultural enchantment with nature. It doesn't translate easily into English, but the basic spirit of friluftsliv hides inside us all.' It entails more than simply being outdoors. It concerns interacting with nature and being part of it. This includes an understanding of the elements around, a sense of oneness with them and a resulting serenity and desire for a true meaning in life. According to Leirhaug (2009), 'Ibsen seems to use friluftsliv in contexts related to freedom won through distancing from social expectations, both the physical and spiritual. Nature and the mountain make room for other actions and other thoughts than conventions require.'

Indicators as to why outdoor learning and a love of nature, as promoted in early years, are so important in Norway have been considered by Kristjansson, who identifies aspects of Nordic society that promote this outlook. He cites the child-centeredness of society, for example the Ombudsman for Children system, which designates a commissioner with statutory rights and duties to promote and protect the rights and interests of children and young people (Kristjansson cited in and Wagner, 2006). Gender equality has promoted a need for childcare as parents seek employment, possibly driven in turn by historical necessities that meant mothers have had to participate in supporting farming or fishing in the short season span available. There is also a sense of social community and of caring for others in the community, being equal members of the group and supporting members within it, demonstrated in the strong welfare state arrangements. The Ombudsman for Children, initiated in Norway in 1981 and swiftly followed by other Nordic countries, safeguarded many children's rights and interests, for example by being on the watch for local and global trends that might threaten children's rights and interests or by monitoring legislative propositions and analysing their consequences for children. Kristjansson states, 'Notably among the large Western European nations, only England and Italy are missing from the lists of countries working to establish an office of Children's Ombudsman' (Einarsdottir and Wagner, 2006: 20). There is an emphasis on early childhood as a state in its own right. Children should enjoy their learning and experiences in the present, not simply as part of a pre-determined journey to the next stage.

Strand suggests a dilemma in Norwegian perspectives: 'since Norwegian early childhood education is justified through cultivation of the "good Norwegian childhood," it contributes to the preservation of "Norwegianness." At the same time, such conservatism is challenged by the multicultural' (Strand, quoted in Einarsdottir and Wagner, 2006: 97). Norwegian society is changing from a homogenous ethnic society to an increasingly multicultural community, where children are given independent outdoor experiences and incorporate diverse perspectives of childhood. Strand argues, 'increased globalisation is instrumental in intensifying local and national negotiations about identity particularly vulnerable because living in an era of constant change calls for multiple identities that are able to cope with continual transformations. This includes the "Norwegianness" within early childhood education' (ibid: 96). International discussions and deliberations continue to promote interactions between philosophies, policies and approaches, further enabling a possible convergence of ideas, which are then incorporated into settings and into ever-changing, responsive notions of good practice.

References

Beckley, P. (2012) *Challenges and Resolutions to Early Years Literacy Approaches in Two Selected Sites in Hedmark, Norway and Lincolnshire, England.* Hull: University of Hull

Einarsdottir, J. Wagner, J.T. (eds) (2006) *Nordic Childhoods and Early Education* Connecticut: Information Age Publishing

Einarsdottir, J. and Wagner, J.T. (2006) Nordic ideals as reflected in Nordic Childhoods and Early Education In *Nordic Childhoods and Early Education* Connecticut: Information Age Publishing

Kristjansson, B. (2006) The making of Nordic childhoods In Einarsdottir, J. and Wagner, J.T. (eds) *Nordic Childhoods and Early Childhood Education: Philosophy, Research, Policy and Practice in Denmark, Finland, Iceland, Norway and Sweden* pp. 13–42 Connecticut: Information Age Publishing

Leirhaug, P. E. (2009) *The Role of Friluftliv in Henrik Ibsen's Works* Sogndal: Sogn og Fjordane University College

McLendon, R. (2014) How 'friluftsliv' can help you reconnect with nature MNN: Mother Nature Network: Earth Matters, Wilderness and Resources https://www.mnn.com/earth-matters/wilderness-resources/blogs/how-friluftsliv-can-help-you-reconnect-with-nature

Ministry for Education and Research (2011). The framework plan for the content and tasks of kindergartens. Oslo: The Norwegian Ministry of Education and Research.

Ministry of Education and Research (2014) Early childhood education and care framework Oslo: Gov.no

Ministry of Education (2017) Forskrift om rammeplan for barnehagens innhold og oppgaver https://lovdata.no/dokument/SF/forskrift/2017-04-24-487

Part 4

Wellbeing as a foundation for philosophy

10 Wellbeing for life in the early years

Pat Beckley and Liz Creed

Overview

The chapter considers how an adult's wellbeing stems from experiences in the early years. These experiences may include challenging events, family circumstances, social, emotional and behavioural difficulties or genetic or hereditary factors. Philosophical perspectives are explored and the chapter considers how these factors can influence approaches in practice.

Introduction

Wellbeing has various meanings and includes the mental state of positivity, contentment and a generally happy outlook on life. Problems with a sense of wellbeing in adult life could arise from experiences in early childhood that have a negative impact. Brain development, emotional challenges, social difficulties, language and communication development, health issues and significant events can all affect children's progress and their outlook on life.

Reflections

Consider your own early childhood. Where there any significant events, happy or sad, that influenced your early life and later development?

Think about smells or sights which bring back memories of your childhood. Do they bring happy or sad memories?

How might the events of childhood have affected your later development?

A secure start

A safe and positive environment impacts on a child's first responses to the world and understanding of his or her role in it. Bronfenbrenner's ecological systems theory (1979) organises the contextual environment into five levels, starting with the immediate environment and proceeding through a widening social development to an eventual awareness of the broadest outlook.

Bronfenbrenner suggests that in the inner level, the *microsystem*, infants are influenced initially by their immediate environment – the adults and children around them, such as family members and siblings. In this way the child learns the cultural mores of those who surround him or her, assimilating the means to have any wants and needs satisfied and observing how to communicate with others by assimilating appropriate responses and social mores. There are numerous factors which may affect a child within the immediate circle of experience. Family dynamics may change as a child grows, becoming more or less positive and secure. A child could be treated differently depending on his or her position within the family or group of children. An older child may be expected to take a lead in interactions and decisions while a younger member may be supported by older children; children have either well-established or more challenging surroundings. Genetic or hereditary aspects could also play a part in the development and responses to situations. These initial interactions have huge implications for a future sense of wellbeing, growth and development. A secure and loving environment that nurtures initial explorations of the world can foster an enjoyment and interest in happenings around the child. A well-nourished child has the requisite physical wellbeing to thrive and grow, responding to new experiences.

The growing awareness of a wider environment, or *mesosystem*, occurs when the child becomes involved with such organisations as childcare, early years units, school, church, or mosque. This supports the child in gaining further understanding of others besides those closest to them and in encountering different personalities. Such an awareness can be developed through, for example, home–school activities, where those most familiar to the child liaise with a new group of people, developing positive communication and broadening the exploration of relationships, interactions and different ways of living. This can continue to develop a child's sense of wellbeing, development and growth, at least in circumstances where all those who support the child are similarly involved and care for the individual as a valued person. When this does not occur and there are challenges in the relationship between immediate carers and the wider group, significant difficulties and confusion can arise for the child. He or she must develop survival strategies in order to operate with differing structures and personalities that do not communicate with each other, or that speak in negative terms of the child's experiences – a possibility that influences the child's view of the world and people in it.

In the next widest layer, which Bronfenbrenner names the *exosystem*, children may be affected by another level of experiences, particularly via an adult or child close to them. For example stresses in a job, such as a demanding teaching role or exhausting shift-work pattern, may result in an adult feeling resentful and oppressed. This may, through the structures within the negatively responsive workplace of the adult, give rise to anger that persists even when the adult is not in that stressful place, and which may be vented against those around the adult when they can express their feelings. This could involve negative reactions to the child or to another child, adult or family member. The child would then have to experience negative responses, either directly or as a result or watching the hostile communication to others they love and care about, causing physical and/or emotional damage.

In the *macrosystem* layer children are influenced and affected by the wider society through cultural, political and economic factors. They may experience a sense of wellbeing or fear and anxiety depending on circumstances in the location or country they inhabit. This could vary greatly depending on a broad range of aspects, such as economic growth or uncertainty, political stability or unrest and the cultural responses of others around them. These would influence the child through their developing awareness of their situation, through news, radio and the internet, which could affect aspects of their personality including resilience, motivation and positivity.

The final consideration concerns the *chronosystem*, which involves changes in circumstance or context. This aspect was added later to Bronfenbrenner's system and concerns the process, person, context and time (PPCT). A child may react differently in different contexts; for example, a child may be very quiet and cause concern for their lack of interaction at school yet be too noisy and boisterous at home. Those involved with the child's development need to operate a holistic view of the child, to address any mismatches in perceptions of the child's development: these could indicate that the child is experiencing difficulty in coming to terms with different locations and expectations, such as between staff and parents. These time factors associated with the understanding of surroundings affect children's moral development, the process through which they come to consider and think independently about social structures and the morality underpinning relationships.

Case study

A child came to the childcare facility greatly distressed. His mother was also tearful, but claimed she was anxious about arriving late and had become 'in a state' getting to the setting. The key worker encouraged the boy to enter the setting and see his friends. He told the worker later that his father had shouted at his mother and broken her favourite breakfast plate and cup. The mother was directed to another helper who calmed her and gave her support through advice about organisations she could access. The family were later supported through their difficult and changing circumstances, with the father's workplace having financial difficulties and redundancy looming for the workers.

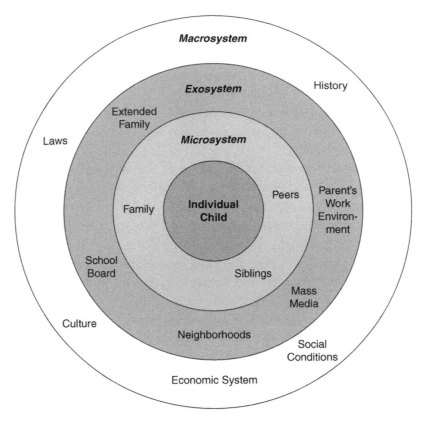

Figure 10.1 Bronfenbrenner's ecological systems theory (Bronfenbrenner 1979)
By Hchokr at English Wikipedia, CC BY-SA 3.0, https://commons.wikimedia.org/w/index.
php?curid=50859630

Reflections

What significant factors have influenced your life?
Have they made changes to the direction you were taking?
With what layer of Bronfenbrenner's theory would they be associated?

Attachments

Children's attachment to their significant adults can foster love or anxiety. Undoubtedly there appears to be a close link between a child's wellbeing and the relationship he or she has with the closest adults. This was highlighted by Bowlby (1953) in his seminal work showing the importance of the mother/child relationship, to enable secure attachment and bonding for the child. Bowlby's work highlighted the need for a secure attachment, for without it a child would have significant difficulties in later life, especially when confronted with challenges to secure relationships (as described in the case study on p. 149) or a lack of a role model to demonstrate appropriate behaviour and interactions to inform a child's later behaviour. The need for a secure attachment to the mother influenced thinking, yet criticism concerned whether it was only the mother who fulfilled this role. Later discussions included a child's main carer, whether it was a parent or adult who held a different relationship with the child, while further findings suggested that children have attachments to a number of significant adults when they are young (Ainsworth, 1971, cited in Grossman et al, 2015).

Reflections

What are your thoughts about Bowlby's theory?

Do you think it has implications for a mother?

If so, what might they be? How might a mother be affected by the knowledge of the theory? Would it influence her decision to work or her choice of childcare arrangements?

What might be the implications of an insecure attachment?

Have you observed insecure attachments, and what happened in your experience of the situation?

Hierarchy of needs

Abraham Maslow (1908–1970) identified a hierarchy of needs (Figure 10.2) applicable to children and adults alike, defining the properties needed to satisfy personal growth and wellbeing. It is often represented as five progressive levels in a pyramid shape.

Maslow's theory of hierarchical needs

The basic needs Maslow identified (1943) were fundamental, *physiological* requirements: food, water, warmth and rest. Still at a basic level, the next stage represented the need for *security and safety*. The second set of needs comprised *belongings and love needs*, such as close relationships (friends and generally being included), followed by *esteem needs*, including the importance of being valued, promoting self-esteem and

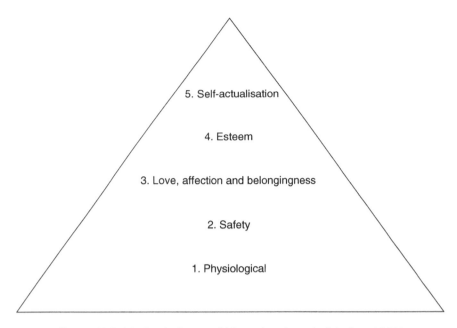

Figure 10.2 Maslow's theory of hierarchy of needs (Maslow 1943)

prestige. Finally, *self-fulfilment needs* identify the importance of self-actualisation; that is, achieving one's full potential and creativity.

Genetic and biological factors

In Bronfenbrenner's Ecological Systems Theory (see p. 150) a person's own biology or growth may depend on factors around them, such as nutritious food, and could be incorporated into the microsystem layer. There is much debate concerning whether a child's development is dependent on nature or nature factors. Professor Colwyn Trevarthen (1931–) highlights the importance of a child's early development. This can have many implications. The brain of every child in every culture goes through the same developmental stages, with children learning in the first five years fifty per cent of everything they will ultimately know. There is an awareness that children are intrinsically motivated to learn, with innate curiosity helping to develop the brain; children also need the right experiences at the right time to develop. The brain is also affected by a child's responses to their surroundings, observing those around them and the environment they live in.

A child's experiences can shape his or her brain, responding to the stimuli around them. Parents and other adults can bring to bear social factors that may influence the child's development and wellbeing: parental views concerning child-rearing, love, bonding, control, neglect and friendships all impact upon the child. Other factors could include security in housing, occupations and whether there are concerns about employment circumstances. Aspects such as the number of siblings, security within relationships and significant changes in family circumstances, for example births, deaths or separation, would also affect the security of the environment. Health issues can also affect a child's sense of wellbeing, whether they affect the child's own health or that of someone close to them.

Burnett (2002) describes American scientist Paul McLean's 'triune brain theory,' which differentiated the reptilian brain, the emotional/limbic brain and the neo-cortex. This theory highlights the crucial nature of wellbeing, suggesting the way and extent to which brain functions are influenced by a child's feelings. The reptilian brain responds rapidly if the individual is in distress or stressed. It maintains life support systems to protect the child (or indeed adult) from a possible threat, enabling a 'flight or fight' response. When this part of the brain is active, the brain is therefore focused on survival strategies rather than learning. A continuous sense of stress would seriously inhibit the child's ability to learn. These implications for the child highlight the need to ensure the child is content and happy if he or she is to fulfil his or her potential. The emotional/limbic brain, meanwhile, handles emotional responses to the world and is linked closely to memories. The neo-cortex area organises the world, accommodating new experiences to previous knowledge. These connections in the brain, or synapses, form strong links between neural cells, developing complex pathways. The synapses are strengthened through stimulation and processing of relevant experiences and stimuli. However, they deteriorate when not used. This has major implications for the environment the child inhabits, entailing that their surroundings and experiences have a direct influence on the development of the brain and consequently the child's learning.

Moral development

There are many philosophical and theoretical bases for emotional and moral development for young children. These concern what is deemed acceptable and unacceptable behaviour.

Sigmund Freud (1856–1939) developed a psychotherapy approach, whereby a patient talks to a consultant to enable insights into problems and discover how to address them. This strategy has links with the talking therapies model used in the NHS. Freud felt there were three interconnected facets to the self: the id, ego and super-ego. The id generated immediate wants and cravings, such as for food. The ego considered others' needs and desires and accommodated the id to a variable extent. The super-ego, developed at around age five, concerned the understanding of right and wrong. Examples of strategies to promote the development of the ego and super-ego are discussed later in the chapter (see p. 158).

Lawrence Kolhberg (1927–1987) identified three levels of moral development – pre-conventional, conventional and post-conventional – with two stages in each. At the pre-conventional level, the *obedience and punishment orientation* has children behave a certain way in order to avoid punishment. The next stage in this level is the *self-interest orientation*, in which children think about what they can get from a situation. At the conventional level, children act first with an interest in *interpersonal accord and conformity*: they try to win approval from others by following social norms. Still within this level, the *authority and social order-maintaining orientation* involves children following rules and insisting that they should be followed. At the post-conventional level individuals adopt first a *social contract orientation* – there is an awareness of the needs of others in the community, which may be greater than personal needs. The final stage within this level concerns *universal ethical principles*: these are deep moral principles, which the person would want to follow. Few reach this stage.

Erik Erikson's (1902–1994) theory considered social and cultural values. He felt there was a series of eight stages of social and emotional development to be passed through from birth to the end of life, each containing conflicts to be resolved. How the person resolved the conflicts would influence the next set of conflicts. Those pertinent to the early years concerned basic trust versus mistrust, from birth to one year/eighteen months; autonomy versus shame and doubt, from twelve/eighteen months to three years; and initiative versus guilt, from three to six years.

Colwyn Trevarthen (1931–) has discussed many aspects of moral development that have influenced practice with young children. His notion of *intersubjectivity* concerned the interactions between the child and adult when they attained a shared meaning. He also notes the importance of musicality in communication, language and music as a means to develop children's understanding and support those who have difficulties, for example through music therapy. Chapter 8 explores this aspect further.

Case study

A circle time activity consisted of discussions of the moral dilemmas contained within many children's favourite nursery stories. A small group of three- and four-year-old children heard the story then considered aspects of it. Were the characters right to behave as they did? What were the good aspects, or the bad? Further knowledge was gained through independent activities linked to the story or through dramatic role-play of events. This was used as an aid for 'hot seating,' where a child chooses a character from the story, explaining his or her views as to why they behaved as they did and considering the consequences of their actions. Children listening also consider the moral dilemma of a situation through the questions they pose. This has been achieved successfully with the youngest children.

Early years practice

Personal, social and emotional aspects of development will be tracked in the early years through appropriate assessments. Initial knowledge of the unique child will arise from liaison with those closest to them, the parents or carers who know most about the child. Further information may be given by organisations with which a child may have come into contact, such as a social worker, health visitor, speech and language consultant or physiotherapist. This information can form the basis of collaboration between those involved in the care and development of the child, to track achievements observed, either at home or in a setting. Early identification of any difficulties is key to addressing possible challenges in the future. This could be through a formal referral, where it is felt appropriate, to gain further support either in the setting or through other agencies, or through an informal note to track a child's progress carefully to identify any underlying problems. As emphasised by Conkbayir and Pascal (2014) 'The message then is clear – the types of environment, and particularly the socio-emotional environment, created for children in their early years is crucial in providing a strong foundation that will start them off on the best trajectory, personally and professionally' (p. 186).This has implications for the environment provided for the child in the earliest stages of his or her life.

The adult working with young children can inform their practice by understanding the philosophies and rationale for the various activities and strategies planned to support children's development. Bronfenbrenner's Ecological Systems Theory (Figure 10.1) leads to an acknowledgement of the importance of the child's first surroundings; positive interactions are therefore crucial to help children build an understanding of their place in the world. These interactions could be with a parent, male or female, or a childcare worker. Organisations involved in young children's care and education typically use a key worker system, whereby an assigned adult will learn about the child as an individual, demonstrating Bronfenbrenner's emphasis on the importance of a stable, safe and secure relationship within the close environment. The child can respond positively to the known adult. The secure emotional environment of a home or childcare base also has importance as a means for the child to learn about the world, providing a safe area for the child to become familiar with and explore.

Further explorations can occur when the child learns about the wider world through such experiences as visits to the shops or accessing a nursery. Children learn about interactions with others through play or communication with others. This can be aided where adults carefully consider the transition between venues, for example home and nursery or childcare or school. The adults in the environment must consider and possibly adjust their planning to accommodate the needs of the children entering a new venue. In early years practice, partnerships between nursery, early years unit or school should have a demonstrable smooth sharing of values to support the child across the different venues.

Reflections

Consider the transitions needed in a child's early life.
How can they be supported to enhance the transition for the child?
What would support entail and who would need to be contacted?

Case study

A child living with a foster carer was visiting the local children's home one weekend. He had difficulty focusing on his work at school and sat alone while he reflected on the tasks given. Discussion with him revealed that he was afraid to attend the children's home, having heard (from others who had not attended it) stories of difficult times and happenings that might occur if he went. He was especially concerned about the possible loss of his 'case' (a blue lunchbox containing all his treasures). It took careful reassurance and contact with the children's home to alert them of his needs before he arrived. He returned to school the following Monday full of excitement over the activities he had been able to participate in and the new friends he'd met.

As the child grows care can be taken to support them as they learn more about the community they live in, giving them wider perspectives on life. This can be incorporated into activities through learning about the history, place names, routes, buildings, parks and other features which make up the area. It is a way of developing children's knowledge of the workings of society and can be used as a means to learn about how systems work, such as roadways, garages and shops. How can members of the community such as grandparents or those holding key roles (e.g. river boat pilots, firefighters, police officers), following safeguarding procedures, be invited to share their experiences.

It may be difficult to be aware of the effect stresses in the workplace have in the home environment. The person causing the discomfort may be so wrapped up in events at work that they are unaware of the effect it is having on those around them. There are many facilities which can help in these circumstances, for example the NHS talking therapies which support individuals to gain knowledge of their actions and the effect it is having, and to carefully consider how to change their behaviour and control their frustration and anger.

Children can be upset by events they observe in the wider context, for example a bombing on the news. It is important to provide reassurance after these events and help children to feel safe by reinforcing that they are with a safe key person who cares for them and are in a secure environment which will not harm them.

Bowlby's effect on practice

Bowlby's work on attachment led those involved in the care and development of babies and young children to reconsider their positions towards their care, either by reaffirming or disagreeing with his position. Bowlby highlighted the need for strong childcare by the mother from the beginnings of a child's life. This would involve daily affirmative interactions with the child, through caring for their needs (appropriate clothing, food and drink) and stimulating them through activities and experiences to engage and delight their senses, demonstrating love towards them.

Factors that impact on the parent then will also influence the child's sense of well-being. Worries about employment, housing and poverty will indirectly cause the child to also worry, picking up on and responding to the anxiety, concerns and possible anger of the adult. A parent who has a negative outlook will transmit this to the child through communication, either verbal or non-verbal.

> ## Case study
>
> A child was abandoned one summer afternoon by her mother in a busy park. She was left with some chips to eat, sitting on a park bench, and told to wait there. She waited the rest of the afternoon and into the evening when it was getting dark. A passer-by noticed the girl crying and came to help. She reported the incident to the police who got in touch with relevant agencies, who organised care for her. During her life she received counselling but was unable to secure lasting relationships as she always doubted her partners' commitment to her, fearing they would leave her. Others were driven away through her constant need for reassurance and anxiety about where they were. She suffered from bouts of depression when memories of that fateful day when she was isolated and abandoned returned.

Key workers

Bowlby emphasised the importance of the mother as an attachment figure for the child, but his work has significant implications for the key worker too. Interactions were shown to have a crucial impact on the child's responses and outlook on their surroundings and the people in them. These experiences were deemed to be determinants for future success in life and ability to interact positively with others, gaining resilience and emotional strength through the foundations built in those early years. Lack of these positive factors was felt to determine to some extent a person's future, predicting possible financial insecurity, unemployment, education short of one's full potential and inability to form lasting relationships. Accepting Bowlby's work would thus affect the behaviour of the adult, knowing that actions and experiences observed by a small child would have a lasting effect on the child and be retained, subconsciously or consciously, into the future. These early experiences would form pathways of behaviour and expectations throughout the child's life, unless the child realised the pathway and wished to change it.

Genetic and biological factors in practice

Children are unique and have their own personal genetic and biological profiles. Health challenges that might require further support could be identified at birth, the two-year check, through a diagnostic assessment on entry to a childcare facility or school or through a referral following a visit to the doctor. Individual plans may be devised, including ways to support the child's development and any possible intervention strategies, for example daily foot and ankle exercises to encourage mobility if recommended by a medical consultant. The further support could address any element of the Early Years Foundation Stage (EYFS) framework, including consideration of such aspects as autism, or could concern a specific health issue such as haemophilia, diabetes or asthma.

Moral development in practice

Freud's ideas can be accommodated in practice through communication and attention to the language used with children and adults. This can be promoted through the general organisation and management of early years settings during play, either adult-led or independent, child-initiated play. Children use play as a means to recount their experiences, assimilating and making meaning from them.

Kolhberg's ideas could influence environments for young children in a variety of ways. Children can be encouraged to think about their situations and those of others, to promote empathy. Thinking about moral rules can be planned into frameworks for daily interactions and ways of living, for example in a setting adults and children together could devise rules, with discussion about why it is important to have rules, their impact on everyone there, the need to create a welcoming space for all to live in, and what basic rules might be agreed upon. Children can then think about what is important when working together so that everyone can have a sense of wellbeing. Formulating rules together will greatly promote the bonding between members of the group and will also increase the likelihood of children adhering to them, as they chose them in the first place. Thus the basic way of living is agreed upon, to support the wellbeing of all.

Further moral development can be enhanced through activities planned to encourage thinking about the rights and wrongs of situations. This could involve rewards for achievements, such as helping another, or time to think when something negative has occurred and discussion about how that might be redeemed. Routines can also be incorporated into daily practice to encourage consideration of others, for example games which involve sharing, taking care of others (such as serving others at snack time), demonstrating politeness, turn-taking when accessing an activity or resources, and showing thanks and gratitude towards others for kindnesses they may show. A 'buddy' system can be introduced, where a child is asked to work with another, to be a friend to them and help them, perhaps if they are new to the setting. There are other ways of promoting care through the 'buddy' system such as having an area a child can visit if they want company, with designated buddies there to help when they see a child in that area. Maintaining an organised environment and encouraging children to collect the resources or belongings they need, then tidy them away, likewise promotes respect for the environment and others who share the space. Children can be encouraged to think about the environment and offer suggestions (which may or may not be used) to develop the environment they access; for example, children can suggest colours to be used or displays created. Specific activities can be introduced to promote aspects of moral development, such as empathy, through a myriad of tasks, as discussed in the case study earlier based on traditional nursery stories.

To accommodate Erikson's theory adults would need to be consistent around the child, enabling trust to develop through the child's knowledge that mores will be adhered to and not changed on a whim. Children's autonomy would need to be accommodated within the framework of behaviour for the home or setting, to enable the child to have confidence in what he or she did, particularly independently, and to ensure he or she was not ashamed or in doubt. This would further boost the child's confidence and self-esteem to use initiative in their play, without anxiety or guilt about behaving inappropriately and experiencing guilt.

Trevarthen highlighted the powerful impact that interactions between the child and adult have in wellbeing and learning. According to Conkbayir and Pascal (2014, p. 98) 'It is now recognised that within hours, a baby is keen to engage in interactions and be social with those in their immediate environment.'

In effect the significant adult or adults in a child's early life and its surroundings – and how they interact with the child – make up the child's world and the wellbeing he or she experiences.

References

Beckley, P. (2012) *Learning in Early Childhood* London: Sage
Bowlby, J. (1953) *Child Care and Growth of Love* London: Penguin

Bowlby, J. (1969) *Attachment: Attachment and Loss* Vol. 1 New York: Basic Books

Bronfenbrenner, U. (1979) *The Ecology of Human Development: Experiments by Nature and Design* Cambridge, M.A: The President and Fellows of Harvard College

Burnett, G. (2003) *Learning to Learn: Making Learning Work for All Students* Carmarthen: Crown House Publishing Ltd

Conkbayir, M. Pascal, C. (2014) *Early Childhood Theories and Contemporary Issues* London: Bloomsbury Publishing Plc

Department for Education (2017) *Statutory Framework for the Early Years Foundation Stage: Setting the Standards for Learning, Development and Care for Children from Birth to Five* London: Department for Education

Grossmann, K. Bretherton, I. Waters, E. Grossmann, K. (2015) Maternal Sensitivity: Mary Ainsworth's Enduring Influence on Attachment Theory, Research and Clinical Application Abingdon: Routledge

Hchokr at English Wikipedia, CC-BY-SA 3.0, https://commons.wikimedia.org/w/index.php?curid=50859630

Maslow, A. H. (1943) A theory of human motivation *Psychological Review* 50 370–396.

Adults working with young children

Pat Beckley

Overview

The chapter explores the work and theories of key early years thinkers and educationalists, including Pestalozzi, Owen, Froebel, McMillan, Dewey, Steiner and Montessori, who developed a philosophical approach to working with babies and young children. These are discussed in terms of their influence on others to establish good practice. The chapter considers a variety of teaching styles, including the importance of the key worker role; it looks at adult-led learning, child-led learning and a child's independent learning; and it considers children's transitions and continuous development. It also raises possible challenges for early years practitioners such as accountability, target setting and the variety of qualifications available.

Introduction

Early years practitioners and those involved in early years have one of the most powerful roles in the country. They shape the futures of the young children they are supporting. How can this be possible? No doubt those who are part of this field will readily understand this notion. Young children will be influenced by the care and education they receive, which will remain with them, either subconsciously or consciously, for the rest of their lives (see Chapter 10 for more on this aspect). The environment surrounding the child, organised by the parent, carer or other person responsible, is created by an adult. Interactions from the adult support the child's learning. This encourages activity in the child's developing brain, strengthening synapses which support understanding and allowing links to be made between aspects of knowledge. The environment the adult creates and establishes can influence children's learning capacity. If the child feels safe, loved, happy and secure and has access to resources that allow exploration and discovery it promotes brain activity. The adult ensures those factors highlighted in Maslow's hierarchy of needs (see Chapter 10) are present so that children can benefit from the stimulation created by the adult. What can key theorists inform us about good practice in supporting all of this?

Pestalozzi (1746–1827)

Johann Heinrich Pestalozzi formed his philosophical ideas through visits with his clergyman grandfather in Switzerland to parishioners living in poverty and by observing the conditions of the children there and in the schools he subsequently arranged and led. His ideas were based on a four-sphere concept of life and on the premise that human nature was essentially good. The spheres consisted of an 'inner sense,' which entailed the satisfaction of basic needs resulting in inner peace and spiritual contentment; home and family; individual self-determination and employment; and relationships with society. He emphasised the holistic nature of development and that every aspect of a child's life contributed to his or her personality, character and reason. His ideas continue to flourish through organisations such as the British charity Pestalozzi International Village, as well as in nursery teacher training in Berlin, postgraduate teacher training in Zurich and Kinderdorf Pestalozzi in Switzerland, which supports children from war-torn areas of the world.

Owen (1771–1858)

Robert Owen was a philanthropist who sought to provide his workers with what he considered equality of workload. He did not employ children under ten and those 10–12 years worked no more than six hours a day. In 1816 he built a school at New Lanark, the site of his business interests including a mill works. The school was termed the Institution for the Formation of Character and provided education while its pupils' parents worked. Owen was influenced by Pestalozzi's ideas on education, particularly those concerning equality and preparation for employment. His schools provided first-hand experiences rather than books, and emphasised the importance of wellbeing, morality, geography, conversation, outdoor provision, music and dance.

Froebel (1782–1852)

Friedrich Froebel was born in Germany. He worked with Pestalozzi for a while and developed his ideas on working with young children: after leading an orphanage for a time he refined his focus to preschool-aged children. He acknowledged the part that active learning plays in children's learning and developed the idea of the Kindergarten, or garden for children. In 1826 he published *The Education of Man*, which discussed children's learning through a play-based approach. He emphasised the crucial nature of work with parents, as they are children's first educators, who interact with children continually and support language development. He advised that those working with young children should use observations to gain knowledge of them. As with Pestalozzi he highlighted the need for children, including those from poor backgrounds, to have access to a healthy lifestyle and have access to the outdoors. He arranged for children to participate in cultivating their own vegetable and produce gardens. Froebel designed educational resources to enhance children's learning: these he characterised as 'gifts' for babies and toddlers, such as balls or wooden shapes to play with and reflect upon, and 'occupations' for older children, consisting of activities through which children could gain knowledge of the properties of the resources.

In Germany at Froebel's time children did not have rights and often worked in difficult situations, such as in mines. His ideas were thought radical and schools following his ideas were banned in Prussia between 1851–1860. In 1908 and 1911 Kindergarten teacher training was recognised in Germany through state regulatory laws.

Reflections

Pestalozzi and Froebel identified the importance of the inner person and self as a way to learn.
Do you agree with this position?
How did these theories differ from those of Skinner?
Do you think there are flaws in the theories?
Pestalozzi, Skinner and Froebel defined many aspects of practice that are currently used. What aspects do you use in your home or setting?

Rachel (1858–1917) and Margaret McMillan (1860–1931)

The McMillan sisters were born in America but came to live in the UK when they were young. In 1894 Margaret was elected onto the Bradford School Board. This experience impacted greatly on her ideas for education improvements, particularly the neglect and preventable illnesses she encountered among the children. She wrote pamphlets for parents about hygiene and campaigned for school medical inspections, school clinics and school meals. In 1902 school boards were abolished and their former remit placed under that of local councils: Margaret at this time joined her sister Rachel in London. Here, she again resolved to improve conditions for children after observing the deprivation experienced by those living in poverty. Margaret became manager of three Deptford schools, at a time when approximately one in five children in Deptford died before they were a year old. Margaret's focus was the education and developmental health of young children and their relationship to home life. In 1905 the Education code stated that under-fives, who had previously been admitted, should not attend school.

The importance Margaret placed upon outdoor living and fresh air as a means to let children experience a healthy lifestyle fostered the opening of a 'girls' night camp' in 1911, followed by the opening of a boys' camp soon afterwards. This led in turn to the opening of an experimental 'baby camp,' which became the Rachel McMillan Open-Air Nursery School. Other nurseries followed and Margaret gave specific instructions about the layout of their environment. The gardens were very important, and, in her opinion, 'the buildings should face south or south east, and in order to have this, the line of the rooms or shelters must be straight, the walls at either end shaped in butterfly form to catch all the sunshine possible' (Shimmin, 2017). Roof lights and moveable walls ensured that there was maximum light and access to the fresh air all year round. These features are broadly retained in McMillan nursery school provision. In 1918, the provision of nursery schools became statutory and Margaret stated,

> a garden-grown humanity cannot be as the humanity of the grime and of the street. It will have spent its first cycle in a place where living things are taken care of so that at least they spring up into things of beauty and colour and perfume. Those who do all this culture work will be cultured. The little gardeners themselves, not the flowers or the vegetables or the trees, will be the glory of the garden.
>
> (Cited in Shimmin, 2017)

Reflections

Has poverty had an impact at your setting or in your experience?
How do you support families through difficult times such as experiences of poverty?

Case study

At a McMillan nursery school in the spring term the teams located in three classrooms worked together to plan forthcoming projects based on a whole-school theme of nursery stories and rhymes. Each class focused on different stories. Resources were prepared and the whole term planning shared with parents. A weekly plan was displayed on the class noticeboard for parents and carers to read when they arrived at the start and finish of the sessions. Most children accessed the provision in either the morning or afternoon, with only those children with particular special needs referred by another agency offered a full-time place. Children played mainly in their classes but staff accessed the outdoor area at times, which was open to the whole school and provided space for children to run and explore. The long corridor with the classrooms leading off it was festooned with bright, attractive displays and information for parents and carers. The atmosphere promoted a welcoming, happy environment where children were eager to be involved and parents shared their children's learning.

Dewey (1859–1952)

John Dewey argued that education and learning are social and interactive processes and the school is a social institution. Children, he wrote, should experience and interact with the curriculum and have a voice in their own learning. He suggested education should be concerned not only with acquiring knowledge but also with learning how to live; that is, through realising one's potential and how to use it for the wider good. He argued that in order for education to be effective it should be delivered with reference to previous experiences, a process that would deepen understanding. He highlighted the need for an active enquiry approach. He reflected upon the approach used for learning and the role the teacher should have in this process. Dewey considered that when education is a one-way process it stifles autonomy. It was, he felt, the responsibility of institutions training teachers to cultivate the attributes he raised. He considered that teachers should equip their students not only to gain knowledge but to develop character, to benefit the community through their intelligence and morality. This would include a love of learning and a desire to communicate it to young children.

Steiner (1861–1925)

Rudolf Steiner, born in Austria, developed a philosophical doctrine based on the importance of thinking, called anthroposophy. He founded the Anthroposophical Society and advocated spiritual growth and a holistic view of education. His views produced such a backlash at the time that there were fears for his safety.

Steiner believed children should experience cycles of activities to consolidate their learning and become reassured about it. Children completed these cycles by the age of seven: he argued that children younger than this should not experience formal education. He founded a number of schools, the first of which became known as the Waldorf school. This led to a worldwide network.

Montessori (1870–1952)

The Montessori approach to educating young children consisted of a child-centred focus, using observations to inform understanding and gain knowledge of children's interests and innate abilities. Its founder Maria Montessori's success led to international recognition in the Association Montessori Internationale (AMI) and the American Montessori Society (AMS). She based her work on observations of children and their explorations with the environment, resources and activities available to them. Her work focused on individuals from birth to age 24, and her educational approaches addressed children aged birth to three, three to six, and six to twelve. It featured a belief that there existed universal, innate characteristics, including such traits as manipulation of the environment and self-perfection.

Montessori carefully structured the learning environment through child-sized furniture, order, and resources made from natural materials such as wood or aesthetic objects. These would be organised in subject areas, within reach of the child and of an appropriate size. Freedom of movement around the classroom space was encouraged. Her management of the early years incorporated aspects such as the grouping of children in mixed-age groups (for example three- to six-year-olds). Children could choose activities from a range of options, a feature of child-centred (not child-*led*) learning. A constructivist pedagogy was used wherein children could discover, as competent beings, and learn through their actions with the resources available. Blocks of time were allotted in which the children had the opportunity to reflect in depth upon the tasks they set themselves. The adult working with the children observed them closely to note their strengths and abilities on which to build. Montessori identified stages in particular aspects of development, such as the acquisition of language (birth to six years); interest in small objects (eighteen months to three years); order (one to three years); sensory refinement (birth to four years); and social behaviour (two-and-a-half to four years). Montessori classrooms for early years children are from two-and-a-half or three to six years and those with a Montessori focus are often called Children's Houses.

Philosophy into practice

At times the cry is heard 'I know about education – I've done it.' Our experiences shape our understanding of learning and teaching and of the strengths and weaknesses within organisations and systems. A particular role model who held significance for the individual may be referred to as a way to approach education. However, reflections on a variety of philosophical stances help in reconsidering personal understandings. Whatever the national policies and guidelines, the way they are implemented is shaped by our beliefs and values. We may not even realise that this is the case until it is pointed out to us or someone with a different view queries it. Pring suggests

> For Dewey…education is this constant transformation of experience, and it is the job of the teacher, being aware of the experiential understanding brought by the

learner into school, to help with that transformation-to introduce the learner to further experiences…which will extend the learner to 'manage life more intelligently.

(Cited in Bailey, 2011: 32)

In early years children will be building on their experiences through interactions with others, initially their parents or carers and later the childminder, key worker or teacher in partnership with parents and carers. Key theories can be considered in terms of personal practice. Naturally, practice may differ widely to suit such factors as the location, context, setting, space or adults involved. A childminder may prepare for different experiences from those in a large school classroom. Similarly nursery settings may differ, from one in a large nursery school to one in a village hall which meets in the morning and has to tidy away in readiness for other groups meeting in the afternoons.

Here are some of the ways key theorists may influence our practice.

Pestalozzi

Pestalozzi's philosophical approach bears many similarities to current approaches. The importance of the home and family links with Bowlby and Bronfenbrenner's emphasis on the importance of the mother and the close circle surrounding the child. It highlights the need to work in partnership with parents and carers and the role of the key worker as a significant person in a child's developing knowledge of people. Independent learning and self-regulation feature, as does an understanding of the community and culture.

Owen

Owen's legacy remains in his many ideas that resonate with providers of care and education for young children. The format of this book bears some resemblance to Owen's wish for a suitable rationale for learning, in that it incorporates the importance of music, a knowledge of other cultures, opportunities for first-hand, active learning, the love of the outdoors, wellbeing and moral development – although perhaps not his preference for an absence of books!

Froebel

Froebel emphasised outdoor learning and opportunities to encourage children to be active and healthy, and to cultivate their own produce in the garden. This is an increasingly fundamental aspect of early years provision where children learn to grow vegetables and fruit and are active in their learning outdoors. His partnerships with parents as a key factor in children's development resemble current policies. His promotion of discovery and understanding through play with resources is the basis of many UK settings' approaches.

McMillan

The McMillan sisters' legacy shares a concern for children's health and welfare and can be compared to Maslow's hierarchy of needs, whereby children's basic needs should be met before they can learn. Their concern for disadvantaged children remains relevant today. Their consideration of an appropriate learning environment posed relevant questions for suitability for young children; this concern continues as ideas about the most appropriate environment change to accommodate new initiatives such as the incorporation of technological tools.

Dewey

The holistic view of education and learning raised by Dewey is relevant to current practice. His advice for training teachers is laudable and remains an appropriate guideline for practice. His notion of preparation for employment links to assessments to secure progress and be of benefit to society.

Steiner

Steiner's legacy includes the importance of active learning, particularly at a young age, and a holistic view of education.

Montessori

Montessori noted the importance of the role of the adult in facilitating children's learning. The learning environment was deemed important, including the use of outdoors, and was designed to be appropriate for children. Settings are carefully considered to gain their optimum use.

The importance of adults working in the early years

Adults working in early years settings have highly complex work, including demonstration as a role model, leading, organising, managing, liaising with parents and carers, collaboration with multiple agencies, working in teams, planning, preparing, assessing, observing, mentoring and coaching, as well as possibly building, fixing, sympathising, caring, learning about health issues and networking. All this occurs when they are deeply committed to the young children at a crucial time of their lives. This period can be a daunting prospect for parents, carers, childminders, nursery assistants and teachers alike.

The role of the adult

Dewey's emphasis on the appropriate training of teachers as future holders of a holistic, 'character-building' role, supporting the preparation for skills and knowledge and the development of the student, is comparable with the Early Years Teacher Status standards (National College for Teaching and Leadership, 2013). They comprise:

1. High expectations which inspire, motivate and challenge children
2. Promote good progress and outcomes for children
3. Demonstrate good knowledge of early learning and the EYFS
4. Plan education.and care, taking into account the needs of all children
5. Adapt education and care to respond to the strengths and needs of all children
6. Make accurate and productive use of assessment
7. Safeguard and promote the welfare of the children and provide a safe learning environment
8. Fulfil wider professional responsibilities

These are divided into sub-sections, for example the first standard entails the following:

1.1 Establish a safe and stimulating environment where children feel confident and are able to learn
1.2 Set goals that stretch and challenge children of all backgrounds, abilities and dispositions
1.3 Demonstrate and model the positive values, attitudes and behaviours expected of children

The standards link many theories concerning the motivation of children (Owen), progress and assessment (Montessori), knowledge of early learning (all theorists), children's needs (McMillan), children's welfare (McMillan) and safety (Skinner), and the professional community (Pestalozzi, Froebel, Dewey). However, all the theorists mentioned in this chapter represent some aspect of the standards within their philosophy.

Professionalism

In Scandinavian countries, such as Norway, early years professionals are instructed in the use of specific pedagogy and practice through programmes that focus on the early years. In some countries or institutions within countries, early years provision forms part of a generic training with sessions incorporating reference to early years. Hevey states,

the traditional and philosophical approach of teacher education was and is very different from that of social pedagogy and focuses more on cognitive and specifically educational aspects of development for children aged 3–7 in the early years (or 5–11 primary phase).

(Cited in Waller and Davis, 2014: 273)

The Children's Workforce Strategy (2005) implemented an Early Years Professional Status to emphasise the social pedagogy approach and highlight training particularly focused on the younger age group. Later, in 2014, the Early Years Teacher Status was introduced, in an attempt to place those working with birth-to-five-year-old children firmly on a par – through qualifications relevant to the age phase taught – with those working with older children. Early years provision has offered a wide base of qualifications for those entering professional work with young children, such as the National Nurseries Examination Board (NNEB) certificate, which provided a sound basis of knowledge and understanding of child development and relevant practice.

This professional stance equips those working with babies and young children with the ability to access knowledge about theoretical models and implement them as they see fit. This is a highly complex undertaking, and includes considering factors such as the locality of the setting, context, aims and values, as well as developing professionally to keep up to date with government initiatives and maintaining evidence to satisfy inspection routines.

Many educationalists, through their observations of their work, have noted that active learning is the most appropriate approach for the youngest children, as highlighted in Owen's ideas. This can be observed by the adult, enabling the assessment and tracking of children's needs and progress and of the suitability of the learning environment provided. Practitioners have a choice of delivery in a formal and informal manner or a mix of the two, depending on the activity proposed. The adult can lead interactions with children or let children take the lead with the adult prompting and encouraging. The role may also include mediation between children to support their understanding of others' points of view, or can involve being a partner, participating in play with the child. Sometimes modelling play is helpful, for example if the children are unsure about a new resource and lack confidence in touching and exploring it.

Approaches to children's activities

A session (for example in phonics) might feature a mix of formal and informal tasks, but different approaches might implement this mix in various ways. The teaching style could for example be adult-led, adult-initiated or child-initiated. Adult-led teaching features an adult leading and structuring an activity throughout, such as may occur during a story-time session. Adult-initiated approaches are those where an adult offers suggestions for the beginning of the session and the children can independently find solutions to the problem or challenge, such as designing a boat that will carry model animals to float on the water tray, or the adult models a pattern and children reproduce it using a variety of materials, for example printed paintings or construction materials. Child-initiated work involves the child thinking to develop an interest and solving a challenge they have set themselves, or using play to further their active learning. Often this type of play would have deep meaning for the child and they may be fully engaged. Many settings have planned routines where the children choose the activity they wish to access and organise their learning, with adults in the setting noting their choices.

Accountability

It is appropriate that adults are accountable for their work and can provide evidence of planning and the resources needed, with consideration for all children. Safeguarding measures should be in place. Accountability for children's progress can be part of the ongoing work so that it does not become a burden. In that way visits from inspectors such as Ofsted can be a celebration of the hard work achieved.

The learning environment

The importance of the learning environment was highlighted by the McMillan sisters and Montessori, with suggestions for appropriately furnished rooms and light space. This would need to be carefully designed, with budgets that may need to be organised over a longer period if items are too expensive at one time.

Resources can be placed at a level where children can comfortably reach them. They can be labelled, pictorially and with the written words, to encourage understanding of print carrying meaning. Boxes can be colour-coded to identify resources used for themes, for example from nursery stories. Resources should be regularly checked for cleanliness and signs of repair needed. However, children may wish to use natural materials that they can give their own meaning to. This can promote their use of their imagination and thinking.

The team can work together to devise a plan for the layout of the space, both indoors and outdoors. Parental help may be available for work on improvements outdoors. Consideration can be given to key areas to be identified in the space, for example a role play area or reading corner, and designed to fit the physical constraints. Care should be taken to identify any difficulties that may arise, such as sand placed too near a doorway, before equipment and furniture are moved.

Figure 11.1 A resource-rich and stimulating environment for children at a childminder's home
Photographed by Pat Beckley at a childminder's home, 2017

A consideration of the learning space must take into account both the physical and emotional aspects of the environment, following Steiner's desire for a holistic approach. The physical environment can be carefully planned to maximise the space and strategies can be devised to ensure no-one is missed (Figure 11.1), through designated responsibility for areas at all times and key workers to track individuals. Strong teamwork can promote swift sharing of any concerns among team members. Children easily identify well-established and effective relationships between adults working with them, which are then reflected in the children's behaviour and feelings of contentment and safety.

Teams may need to work together to identify their shared understandings about early years learning if pressure to prepare children to achieve when they are older impacts upon the learning styles promoted in the setting. Value-added evidence can support assessments of children's progress and outcomes. These can be identified with parents or carers when a child enters a setting or facility, then again when moving to the next stage of learning.

Playing and exploring

Planned, purposeful play along with a mix of adult-led, adult-initiated and child-initiated activities underpins learning and development. Flexible, ever-changing play supports children's cognitive development through their interactions with their surroundings and others. They can relive experiences to help them reflect about what happened, for example in role play or small world representations.

Active learning

Theories discussed earlier note the importance of active learning through exploration and discovery, either independently or socially with peers and adults. Children's abilities and any support needs can be addressed during the independent play. Initial assessments with parents can be used to identify the child's interests, and resources and activities fostered to build on these. Formative assessments can be used to ascertain whether the child is accessing areas of the setting and participating socially. When the child is secure and familiar in the environment further challenges may be posed by the child to extend their learning. They gain a sense of achievement when planning and addressing problems they have set themselves. Areas of learning should be considered, covering activity areas such as water play, a creative area, outdoor moveable toys, open space, climbing, role play, small world, music area, dance performance platform, reading area, large construction, sand area and welcoming area to greet parents and carers as they enter the setting. Through their play children should be able to explore and discover, interact with their peers and adults, gain new understandings, knowledge and concepts, demonstrate resilience and learn positively from their mistakes, develop their interests, initiate their own ideas using resources and natural materials, question and gain information through such resources as technological tools, celebrate achievements and develop their understanding of others while working with them. Displays can stimulate learning, as can the use of interactive walls, including celebrations of achievements from the children's perception of work they feel is of good quality.

Transitions and continuous development

Liaison between adults is crucial to promote children's happiness and foster smooth transitions between home and settings or settings and school. The importance of the home and partnerships with parents are key for successful transitions, and practitioners need to be proactive to manage this arrangement. The change may be difficult for parents too, as it involves a realisation that the child is growing and becoming more independent. If possible, visit the new setting with the child and help them to get to know their new key worker and surroundings. Share knowledge of existing attainment, development and any concerns you may have. It is useful to give the child something to remember the new setting, such as a paper hat or picture.

Reflections

Consider changes made when you were young. How did you feel about them? What transition strategies are in place for the child or children you support?

As suggested at the beginning of this chapter adults involved with our youngest children have a powerful role in effectively supporting their learning and development. It is a complex, demanding, yet highly satisfying and rewarding role.

References

Bailey, R. (2011) *The Philosophy of Education* London: Continuum International Publishing Group

National College for Teaching and Leadership (2013) *Early Years Teachers' Standards* https://www.gov.uk/government/publications/early-years-teachers-standards

Shimmin, A. and staff (2017) McMillan Nursery School: History of the McMillan Sisters http://www.mcmillannurseryschool.co.uk/?p=2078

Waller, T. Davis, G. (2014) *An Introduction to Early Childhood* London: Sage

12 Early years challenges for the future

Pat Beckley

Overview

Future challenges include meeting all young learners' needs, with opportunities for them to use their full potential to meet the needs of changing local, national and international contexts. Meeting these challenges requires a broad framework to allow for independent thinking (see Chapter 5 on children's philosophical thinking) and a willingness to be open to new ideas and ways of working, considering approaches in other countries and adopting those deemed to have a positive impact. Approaches will need constant adjustment to fit the continually changing contexts of future needs, including those concerning technological advances, health, equality and the imperative to offer education for all.

Chapter 1 considered international pressures in political, economic and cultural contexts. This is discussed for possible future challenges which may impact on early years provision and those who are involved in it.

Political challenges

Political rhetoric asserting that we require a world-class education system to ensure children become global citizens directs attention to outcomes for children and international league tables: 'Education is linked to the creation of skills that enable a country to compete in a global economy' (Shields, 2013: 6). Modernisation theories, whereby developing countries would simply need to add new industries to secure progress, began to be queried when taken-for-granted phenomena such as financial stability, mineral and natural wealth (such as forestation) encountered difficulties. Concern was directed toward the quality of life experienced. The 1948 United Nations Declaration of Human Rights stated 'Everyone has the right to education.' The World Conference on Education for All (1990) committed participating countries to provide primary education for all by 2000. The subsequent World Education Forum produced the Dakar Framework for Action, which included as one of its six goals to expand and improve comprehensive early childhood care and education. There are many challenges when implementing these directives, for example cost of provision, staffing requirements, venues, and promotion of the desire for education, especially when children may be expected to work. The registration of births may not be fully accurate in some areas, meaning that a detailed account of children who should be attending is difficult to ascertain. Families may be unable to meet the costs of school clothing and books that may be required. In this way some families may have to choose one child from the family to access the provision, who can later in life help other members of the family through better paid employment.

Applications of the Education for All agenda can vary depending on the viewpoint taken as to why this is being promoted. Such a tension was identified in Chapter 1 and influences policies and practice: for example, education viewed as a source of capital would differ from provision where a Marxist view prevailed, with equality of opportunity in society deemed crucial.

As seen with the different philosophies for early years education and care in England, Norway and Uganda discussed in Chapter 1, political, economic and cultural factors influence what it is expected will be taught and learned, and how this is implemented differs in context. Practice is affected by questions concerning national political agendas, how they have arisen, the policy context and the localities and communities in which settings or other early years provision are placed (with differences for example between rural and urban environments). It is pertinent to query the purposes of education. Is it to enable children to learn basic facts and a dominant language, or to build on their strengths and give them insights into the world around them and their locality? Skills and abilities can be valued equally, with value not accorded simply to mainstream academic styles of learning. For example, in a community visited, families struggled to secure places for their children at university. But after graduating, individuals from this community had difficulties finding graduate jobs in urban areas, and also had not learned the traditional skills, such as fishing or woodcraft, that would allow them to support their home communities and give them a way of living.

Reflections

What are possible educational values for communities?
Are a variety of skills, attainments and attributes valued?
Do you feel some skills are more highly valued than others?
Why might this have happened?

Economic challenges

The world is shrinking more than ever, with global economies, international companies and swift internet communication encouraging debate on education's value for money, outcomes and future prospects. Neoliberal theory gives rise to a notion of competition for jobs and wealth in a 'free-for-all' competition-driven economy. International companies compete for financial superiority, with workers paid to sustain profit margins. Schools, for their part, compete in league tables and demonstrate the 'best' results from their pupils. Stories arise of the exclusion of those who may not achieve such results.

New industries, moving away from a reliance on extensive manpower, seek intellectual knowledge to operate. This global knowledge economy promotes the importance of a highly skilled workforce who can meet its demands. However, the increase in well-qualified individuals can accentuate competition for jobs, driving wages down or prompting a search for alternative training 'on the job,' a possibly cheaper method of acquiring qualifications and a way of regulating numbers training by ensuring jobs are secured prior to training.

Cultural challenges

The extent to which the elite in a society provides a framework for early years provision – such as formal, assessment-driven outcomes for children, which in turn are used to assess the provision, or a focus on the process of learning – depends on the cultural mores of that particular society. 'World culture theory identifies international organisations, such as the World Bank or United Nations, as key agents of globalisation: through their international declarations these organisations embody a 'world culture' that values individualism, democracy and human rights' (Shields, 2013: 75). These key agents of world culture might also include organisations and networks operating internationally, which greatly influence philosophy and thinking in early years practice. Movement of people serves further to disseminate cultural practices; see for example Strand's argument in Chapter 9 (p. 143). Such movement may reflect numerous motivations, such as flight from war-torn areas, education and employment opportunities, international companies or expertise, or displacement. Cultural views will change as different perspectives and understanding seep into existing thinking.

Technological challenges

The explosion of technological advances has transformed everyday life and early years practice. Internet access to research on such subjects as plants, minibeasts or animals is ready available. Staff members, parents, carers and those in other multi-agency organisations can communicate easily through mobile phones. Computer links such as Skype allow us not only to communicate with others around the world but see their location and converse as part of a group, perhaps on opposite sides of the globe. This knowledge about other ways of working and readily accessible information gives a wider dimension to practice and broadens the experiences of the children. Many are 'computer literate' and have access to many technological devices to help them find out about the world. Through relevant apps, they practise skills such as handwriting, mathematics or the use of toys and games (for example Beebots).

Reflections

What technological equipment do you use?
What technological equipment do the young children you know have?
How does the technological equipment support their learning or disadvantage them?

Technology can be a useful tool to support development, or can inhibit it. This is a particularly relevant consideration for practitioners, who can incorporate it into everyday activities as a tool of learning rather than relying on it as a way of maintaining quiet! Children can become reliant on a technological aid almost as a friend, or in place of one. Care must be taken to ensure children are not becoming over-reliant on their technological support, such as an iPad or computer game. Safeguarding measures need to be put in place too to check children can only access appropriate material through the internet.

Adults can help children navigate technological systems, modelling and guiding their use. The devices can be incorporated into adult-led, adult-initiated or child-initiated activities. Technological tools, for example speech and language recognition systems, can be highly effective for children with special needs or to challenge individuals. A useful notion for describing literacy and digital technology is Hill and Mulhearn's (2007) term 'multiliteracies', which highlights the understanding of the potentially multiple means of communication, such as visual or technological understanding. Technological use can be included throughout the curriculum and gives children strong visual clues, for example by using technologies for word recognition or story-telling in literacy, to practise skills in mathematics or colour mixing in art and to promote understanding and knowledge of the world.

Planning can include noting what technology is used in the sessions, how it is used and why. Assessments of individual children can include their progress in technological understanding and skills when using the devices. Many young children use technological devices at home, such as switching on the television, music system or computer game. McLachlan et al. (2013: 177) state, children are entering early years settings with a range of skills, abilities and experiences that children of the past did not have, so teachers of the future need to both understand ICTs, and use them in the classroom if they are going to provide a curriculum that is culturally and socially meaningful to children.

Equality challenges

The understanding of every child as unique supports the notion that each person has differing backgrounds, skills and abilities and is valued in society. Yet some children may experience more challenges than others, which prompts the question of how equality can be achieved. Should those with challenges be given further support to make them equal? What form should this take?

Hill and Robertson (2012) suggest different ways of viewing the situation, including a liberal progressive stance advocating tolerance, mutual respect and multiculturalism; a social democratic approach that seeks to engage in reforms; critical pedagogy aiming to expose how the capitalist society works; or a Marxist or socialist perspective. Yet these stances, whichever is adopted, need to be disseminated into practice at home and in a setting or school. How can this be achieved to ensure equality of opportunities, drawing on individual strengths and abilities? The importance of parental partnerships has been highlighted, for example in Bronfenbrenner's ecological model (1979), and these can be the foundation to ascertain a child's attainment and where further support or resources may be needed.

A review of one's personal philosophy concerning the early years empowers those involved with babies and young children to identify the aims and values for what is being achieved. Initial discussions about a child, undertaken between the adults concerned with that child, can be used to identify the next steps, whatever area of learning these may cover. A high ratio of adults to children enables adults to gain extensive knowledge of each child and the parents/carers. It also facilitates knowledge of the child as an individual and makes it easier to allow the child to follow their interests and learning with the interaction of a knowledgeable adult. To provide this level of support takes time and commitment from the adult, as well as finances. Financial considerations, including resources, can lead to larger groups of children per adult, and reduce opportunities to give individual support. Careful planning needs to be in place to ensure individuals and their need for development are not missed. Needs factors may be wide-ranging and include poverty, support for language understanding, special educational needs, children in care, transition issues, gender, refugees, parental employment challenges or health concerns. Evidence of the rationale for planning for individuals can be noted, and in situations where outcomes-driven agendas are in place, used as a demonstration of how the child is being supported in their learning and development.

An honest, insightful reflection on personal views is required to yield a knowledge of the perspectives held and whether they are inadvertently disadvantaging children. Lack of understanding of different backgrounds, with the strengths and challenges they represent, hinders the ability to support children as individuals, hence the continual desire for a widening professional perspective. The philosophy of the whole setting or school and the promotion of the values inherent in the provision help to provide guidelines and a rationale for the work achieved there, and identify the stance taken by the organisation. Some settings may emphasise specific outcomes to be attained by children and the possibilities they afford for later life, while others may highlight the progress achieved and the individual skills, personal development and learning secured. Hill (2012: 294) notes that, 'with exceptions, and despite the best efforts of many teachers and schools, the hidden curriculum serves, in general, to reproduce the educational, social and economic inequalities in classrooms, schools and society, rather than expose, challenge and contest these inequalities.' Early years providers are possibly in a fortunate position to gain knowledge of their children through liaison and partnerships with families, carers and the community they serve in an attempt to address any inequalities. The matter is complex, for example attempts to address gender inequality may need careful negotiation and sensitive collaboration.

Health challenges

Children are exposed to views about health from their earliest years, and patterns of behaviour for health are also established early. Healthy nutrition habits along with physical activity support children's wellbeing and physical development. Conversely, lifestyles featuring hurried snack meals, sedentary schedules and a lack of physical activity can lead to obesity, while a lack of nutritious food can lead to reduced energy and decreased physical and cognitive ability. Sedentary lifestyles, pressure to attain certain outcomes and poverty can all weaken physical development and the sense of wellbeing. When these patterns of behaviour become established it is difficult to forge new ways of living; they could thus lead to lasting harm, such as a lack of calcium, resulting in rickets and the challenges in later life this would cause.

Early years professionals

Those working or involved with babies and young children, whether professionals or parents/carers, can change their own practice as wider perceptions and changing views of early years practice evolves in light of international initiatives and fresh ideas. Observing practice in another country and studying the policies, practice and approaches to learning and the underlying philosophy provides a different perspective. Daily routines and strategies can be seen from another angle. For example, to an observer from England, daily safety routines that involve passing through locked gates and boundary fences, or a wall surrounding a compound with an armed security guard at the gate – all features of the Ugandan setting discussed here – may cause reflections before even entering a facility. Various approaches to early education, reflecting the cultural mores of the society they represent and the context in which the setting is situated, may be most suitable for the community each setting serves. Nevertheless, aspects of practice can be shared and adapted as appropriate to meet local needs and interwoven into existing practice in another country. This intercultural dialogue can benefit all countries involved, as each reflects on their existing practice and considers the origins, strengths and weaknesses of their own approach. In this way policies and practice can respond to current initiatives and requirements.

Reflections

Do you have links with a setting in another country?
What aspects of practice are similar between the two settings?
What aspects of practice are different?
What are the factors that cause the similarities and differences?
Are there any aspects you might change in your home or setting after your reflections about a different practice?

Convergence and trends

According to Shields (2013: 76), 'researchers are asking why education systems throughout the world are converging on a common set of policies and practices, examining the effects of international organisations in isomorphism, and questioning the future of the nation-state in a globalised world.' How does this notion align with early years philosophy and practice? Certainly key issues appear to be arising throughout the world to be experienced by those involved in early years. Philosophies, policies and practice are based on contextual foundations and are therefore assimilated in different ways in one country from the one in which they arose; consider for example the variable desire for outdoor learning within the cultures in England and in Norway (see Chapter 9). Discussions suggest the idea of a holistic view of early years provision, to be implemented according to attitudes that depend on context. Despite concerns over the process of education and with care for young children deemed to be of paramount importance in some countries, for example in Nordic regions, assessments to provide evidence of children's outcomes seems to be growing in popularity. There is also an increasing demand to have qualified staff working with the age group. Even certain particular early years programmes for children appear to have been disseminated world-wide, for example popular phonics programmes or Maths Mastery. Aspects of good practice, such as outdoor learning in Nordic countries or the Reggio Emilia approach, have been accommodated into settings elsewhere. Early years practice is constantly evolving and will require practitioners to have a professional stance, critiquing philosophical approaches and implementing them to serve the best interests of the children in their care.

Further reading

Bailey, R. (2011) *The Philosophy of Education: An Introduction* London: Continuum International Publishing Group

Miller, L. Cable, C. Devereux, J. (2005) *Developing Early Years Practice* London: David Fulton Publishers Ltd

References

Bronfenbrenner, U. (1979) The Ecology of Human Development: Experiments by Nature and Design Cambridge MA: Harvard University Press

Hill, D. (2012) Theorizing politics and the curriculum. In Hill, D. Robertson, L.H. (eds) *Equality in the Primary School: Promoting Good Practice Across the Curriculum* London: Continuum International Publishing Group

Hill, S. Mulhearn, G. (2007) Children of the new millennium: research and professional learning in practice *Journal of Australian Research in Early Childhood Education* 14 (1) 57–67

McLachlan, C. Fleer, M. Edwards, S. (2013) *Early Childhood Curriculum: Planning, assessment and implementation* Cambridge: Cambridge University Press

Shields, R. (2013) *Globalization and International Education* London: Bloomsbury Publishing Plc

United Nations (1948) *The Universal Declaration of Human Rights* New York: United Nations

Concluding comments

Adopting a philosophical approach towards involvement with babies and young children provides some understanding of what is being achieved and how. Through such an approach, consideration can be given to the purpose of the provision. Is it a business, a profit-making machine to produce economically viable returns? Is it a provider where children become acquiescent members of society? Is it part of an international, corporate facility, or a setting following a key theoretical stance? These are possible examples, but thought can be given to your involvement with young children: you can query the elements that make up what is involved in your provision. If there is an awareness of an underlying rationale then further thought can be given to how provision is delivered to promote that philosophy, whether it be formal or informal, adult-led or child-initiated. The amount of planning required concerning opportunities, space, time, resources and recording would depend on separate deliberations about how important each of these factors is. A setting may adopt a focus on the child: the individual progress and outcomes he or she makes may be a centre of focus for practice. Alternatively, in a socially constructed view of development, the concern may be for the child to be an active participant. According to Dahlberg et al. (2007: 55), 'From a postmodern perspective, there is no absolute knowledge, no absolute reality waiting 'out there' to be discovered … the world and our knowledge of it are seen as socially constructed and all of us, as human beings, are active participants in this process.' Those involved with babies and young children can build on their existing understandings, changing and reflecting on them as they deem appropriate. Practitioners' wider knowledge and understanding of differing ways of working gained by considering international perspectives and new initiatives enable them to make professional decisions; teamwork allows them to share thoughts and ideas about what is happening and how this impacts upon the children.

The cry for independent-minded children who can face the unknown challenges of the future is currently commonplace, in the face of uncertainty and with the prospect of a postmodern new order. Yet children's independence, promoted by a philosophical understanding of what they are doing and why, can only serve to enhance their wellbeing and make them agents of their own destiny. Activities promoting philosophical ideas, either through discussions or role play or based on resources, can help a child to think about what they are doing and why, taking ownership of their actions. A widening knowledge and understanding about their world and those more distant from them, cultivated through links with others, gives children further insights into different ways of living, care for those around them and the environment they live in. It incorporates sustainability as a measure to continue to care for the surroundings and to benefit the rest of the planet. There are many references to children becoming part of a global economy and world citizens, for example in the UK Callaghan's Ruskin College speech of 1976 or Tony Blair's in 2005. Further knowledge of a widening, international world supports young children to gain an understanding of diversity, starting with the children and adults they know and expanding to a widening awareness of the diverse nature of the communities we live in. Children will also gain a depth of understanding about the mores of society and what is appropriate. Very young children have a sense of 'fair play' and justice which, when nurtured, can provide excellent foundations for their emotional and social development and can benefit those around them. Consideration of their values, of how and why they behave in certain ways, can only serve them well in future interactions with others and in generating their own ethical and moral codes for living. The philosophical approach can be part of their early development and will support them as a means of traversing considerations and challenges throughout their lives.

References

Dahlberg, G. Moss, P. Pence, A. (2007) *Beyond Quality in Early Childhood Care and Education* 2nd ed. London: Routledge

Pound, L. (2011) *Influencing Early Childhood Education: Key Figures, Philosophies and Ideas* Maidenhead: Open University Press

Index

Note: **Bold** page numbers indicate tables, *italic* numbers indicate figures.

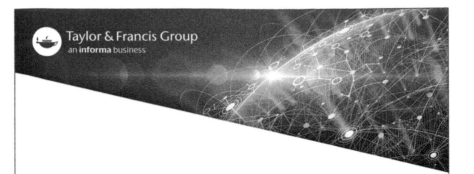